As someone who has spen[t] growth and development of some of the top CEOs and Key Executives in the world, I know how to spot a gem when I see one! I find *Truly Rich* to be an excellent resource for people looking to understand how to get rid of the baggage we carry with us around money and wealth and start stepping more confidently into their financial future.

—**ANTHONY M. FLYNN,**
*Founder & CEO, AmazingCEO*

I wish I had this book in my early thirties as my income was really starting to grow! It is completely different from any other book on finances in that it isn't a guide on how to *make* money, but a guide for how to *manage* your income in a way that is healthy both financially and emotionally. It's perfect for women who are intimidated by finances and are ready to truly get ahead and be independent and finan-cially secure.

—**KATE UHRY,**
*Photographer & Business Owner, Kate Uhry Photography*

All readers will see themselves in Nicole's inspiring and enlightening book, either as an Everyday Person who needs to embrace the 10 Critical Habits, or as a Truly Rich Person who needs to be intentional about maintaining their emotional and financial wealth and leaving a strong legacy.

—**ANNE C. EWERS,**
*President & CEO, Kimmel Center, Inc.*

Nicole Perkins' enlightening new book, *Truly Rich*, lays out an actionable blueprint for financial independence gleaned from decades of thought-provoking insights and measurable strategies. Nicole's 10 Critical Habits are not only effective for professionals at every stage of their careers, they are truly empowering.

—ED DANDRIDGE,
*Vice Chair, The Executive Leadership Council*

Nicole's unique insights into the world of wealth will help anyone improve their relationship with money. Her expert guidance through the emotional obstacles on the road financial freedom is exceeded only by laughter and tear-inducing anecdotes from her personal journey to become Truly Rich. A must-read!

—BRENDAN BILES,
*Investment Banking Analyst, Portico Capital Advisors*

Nicole Perkins has lessons to give! There are lessons from years of professional experience helping wealthy clients. However, it is her personal story, and her willingness to share her struggles and her triumphs, that make this book such a heartfelt, helpful, and enjoyable read. I highly recommend it for everyone trying to improve their relationship with money and, thus, improve their lives.

—DR. ROSINA S. MILLER,
*Director, Stanford in New York*

If you want to increase your understanding of personal wealth and wealth building, there are lots of books you could read. However, if you want to truly discover the habits and actions necessary to build and sustain wealth, this is the only book you need. Nicole does a fantastic job of outlining the basics while also underscoring the intangibles in a way that makes the entire process feel wholly attainable. No matter your current income or career trajectory, if your future goals include generational wealth building, then your personal library needs to also include this book.

—**ANGELA BOSTICK,**
*Chief Marketing & Communications
Officer, The Wharton School*

Nicole Perkins' inspiring book, *Truly Rich*, delivers invaluable insight and practical step-by-step guidance to creating financial well-being which is an essential part of a balanced, meaningful, and rewarding life.

—**DR. KAREN PERKINS,**
*Psychologist*

*Truly Rich* provides readers with a handful of valuable financial tools that are easy to digest, practical to implement, and beneficial to people of all financial backgrounds. Nicole's cash flow management techniques and budgeting strategies immediately improved the way I manage my money.

—**CULLAN GILROY,**
*2021 Summa Cum Laude Graduate of
the University of Pennsylvania*

As a result of reading the insight from Nicole Perkins's many years of extensive guidance of an array of clients, I now truly comprehend that financial success comes down to a psychological and emotional relationship to money itself.

—DIANE MYLES,
*Master Pilates Instructor/Pilates Practitioner*


In *Truly Rich*, Nicole translates lessons learned from her remarkable career advising wealthy clients, and her own personal experience, into thoughtful, practical habits for achieving financial confidence and security. Through real-world examples, Nicole examines the strategies used by people who understand and are comfortable with their finances and empowers her readers to implement these same strategies in their lives. *Truly Rich* is a smart book for people who want to take control of their finances.

—PETER MUNDHEIM,
*Managing Director and Counsel, Stone Point Capital.*


*Truly Rich* is a well-crafted and insightful journey that guides the reader through all the important considerations necessary to effectively manage wealth over generations. Drawing from Nicole's deep wealth management experience and expertise along with her personal stories creates an engaging, educational and practical tool that families will benefit from.

—MICHAEL A. COLE,
*author of More Than Money, A Guide to
Sustaining Wealth and Preserving the Family*

Part financial education, part personal development... *Truly Rich* is full of practical ways to have the right relationship with money.

—**JASON A. SNIPE,**
*Principal, Odyssey Capital Advisors*

Nicole Perkins's magic mix of insight, wisdom, and personal reflection provides the practical strategies as well as the inspiration to apply her 10 Critical Habits to become Truly Rich. You won't want to miss this invaluable guidebook to ensure your financial security and success!

—**DEBBIE EPSTEIN HENRY,**
*Founder, DEH Consulting, Speaking, Writing and Podcast Host, Inspiration Loves Company*

A wonderful book on how our relationship with money drives whether or not we become wealthy. Each chapter is filled with thought-provoking stories on how to build wealth soundly and simply, while at the same time enjoying the ride. Nicole's real-life experiences resonated so much with my own that I bought four copies for my young adult children.

—**CHARLES P. GARCIA,**
*best-selling author of A Message from Garcia: Yes, You Can Succeed*

# TRULY
# RICH

## An Insider's Guide to Building
## FINANCIAL and EMOTIONAL
## Wealth

# NICOLE PERKINS

WEST
PUBLISHING

*To my parents, Gail and Henry Perkins, who gave me everything I needed and more.*

*To my husband, Giorgio Piatti, who supports me in everything I do.*

*To my children, Maya, Alina, Claire, Chiara, and Gio, who give me inspiration & motivation everyday.*

# CONTENTS

# INTRODUCTION

A lot of people seem to be getting rich these days, and in unconventional ways. Some, like Steve Jobs, Mark Zuckerberg, Bill Gates, and others, started highly successful businesses without needing to obtain a college degree; some, like Larry Page and Jeff Bezos, built multibillion-dollar companies in their garages, and some recent startups have sold for billions of dollars, making their founders rich overnight. We do not have to search far to see CEOs of Fortune 500 companies making millions—if not billions—of dollars. Social media has fueled a new industry of influencers, some who earn from $100,000 to $1,000,000 per post! Even during the Covid-19 pandemic, the number of millionaires in the world increased by 5.2 million, driven by a rise in stock and housing prices, as well as actions taken by governments and central banks to mitigate the economic impact.[1]

These rich people seem to have effortlessly landed in the kind of life and wealth most people can only dream of, their riches giving them financial freedom, affording them exceptional experiences and providing a life of happiness.

However, some rich people can also feel compelled to "keep up with the Joneses" as they wrestle with how much is enough, fear losing their money, make poor financial decisions, and feel unhappy despite their riches. They may be rich in the financial sense, but their emotional richness is significantly depleted.

> Wealth can be a mixed blessing, providing power, independence, pleasure, and protection, but also bringing serious responsibility and emotional issues. I've seen this struggle between financial and emotional richness in many of my clients. For the last twenty-five years I have worked in the financial industry as a business attorney, a trust and estate attorney, a wealth management advisor, a senior executive of a Fortune 500 financial company, and a partner in a wealth management RIA. Over these years I have advised hundreds of millionaire and even billionaire clients, serving as their attorney, personal financial advisor, or as the trustee over their trusts and investment portfolios.
>
> As an insider in this industry, I have had a front-row seat to a wide range of relationships people have with money, from disastrous to successful and everything in between. It is easy to see what financial wealth looks like, but harder to understand what *emotional* wealth looks like.

Money comes and goes in the real world. Outside circumstances impact your financial situation no matter how rich or how smart you are. Emotional wealth means having the power to achieve a sense of fulfillment and well-being regardless of your financial wealth.

But what about those people who are doing everything they can to achieve financial success and live the American

Dream? The people whose parents worked relentlessly in their prime, frequently sacrificing their own aspirations so that their children might achieve more. The people who went to college in the hopes of advancing their careers and earning more money. The people who have put in long hours, often working two jobs or going to school at night to get a professional degree.

Some of these folks work as professionals, earn a lot of money, and own a home. These are the people who have made mistakes but who have also had successes. These are the people who have paid their dues, and society told them it should lead to financial success.

Yet so many of these people have much less than they were led to believe they would have, living paycheck to paycheck without financial security and with great frustration, worry, and disappointment. Some did make a fortune only to see it slip through their fingers. Others have ended up less wealthy than their parents and wonder, *How did this happen?*

These are the people who want to better their financial situation, modify old or unhealthy money habits, and build new and necessary habits for long-term success. These are the people I call *Everyday People*. Regardless of their current level of wealth, they are seeking assistance in safeguarding their financial future as well as their happiness.

Of special interest to me are the financial habits of women—especially women of color. As a black woman, I have experienced firsthand the unique challenges around race and gender when it comes to financial and emotional wealth. I have addressed some concerning statistics unique to these groups in the Appendix at the end of this book and encourage every reader to explore this critical topic more.

All Everyday People, of every race and gender, are looking for financial wealth *and* emotional wealth. They want to get off the roller coaster. In other words, they are looking to become what I call *Truly Rich*. I wrote this book for them.

## CHAPTER ONE

# AN UNCOMMON RELATIONSHIP

Ruth is a 40-year-old mother of two and a doctor. She enjoys spending time with her family in their lovely suburban home. Ruth and Buck have what most people would consider a typical relationship. She admires, respects, and is perhaps a little in awe of Buck and what they might be able to accomplish together.

Their relationship, though, can be challenging. Ruth rarely expresses herself or specifically defines what she wants or needs from Buck. She assumes he will just know. Buck is incapable of knowing what Ruth does not share but indeed does what is possible to meet most of what appears to be Ruth's needs. They go with the flow and do not think too much about their relationship. They just enjoy life and trust that their future is bright.

But when faced with change or unanticipated circumstances, Buck is not as dependable as Ruth expects him to be. When this happens, Ruth becomes concerned about their stability and whether Buck is truly dedicated to being in the relationship for the long haul. When their relationship hits these rough patches, Ruth diligently works to address the issues as best she can, adjusting her own goals and lowering her expectations of Buck.

After a while, things usually get back on track, and Ruth feels safe in her relationship again. She feels happy, and her expectations of Buck begin to grow once more. Unfortunately, Ruth and Buck never examine their relationship and therefore never know when, why, or if the relationship will hit another snag. These snags are not ideal, but they are also not devastating, so Ruth just accepts what she considers to be the reality of relationships. That is just how they work.

Just next door, however, Nick is not in a healthy relationship with Penny. He is 52 years old and works as a private school teacher. Nick was married and divorced early in his life before recently remarrying. Nick is continually worried that Penny will abandon him when he needs her the most and that their relationship will collapse at any moment.

Nothing could be further from the truth, yet that is how Nick feels. As a result, he typically ignores Penny and focuses on his work as a protective mechanism. He knows Penny is trustworthy, and he wants them to be happy together, but he is terrified to let that happen. Given how much Penny gives to the relationship, it is remarkable that Nick makes no attempt to comprehend his inexplicable feelings for her. He hopes that things will improve over time.

Meanwhile, two doors down, Tamara and Ben are in a strong and healthy relationship. They frequently discuss their relationship goals and make plans to achieve them.

They take steps to ensure they will stay together forever. Like any relationship, they have ups and downs, but they weather those ups and downs well through their attention and preparedness. Their relationship is not all work, though. They enjoy each other immensely. However, they also know their relationship alone is not the only thing that will fulfill them. For instance, Tamara gets additional and needed fulfillment from her family, valued friends, work, and travel. As a result, Tamara and Ben are set for a loving, long, and prosperous future.

Before you check the book cover to see if you accidentally picked up a couples therapy book, let me explain what is going on here.

Buck, Penny, and Ben are not real people, although the relationships they have with Ruth, Nick, and Tamara are all too real. Buck is a common slang word for the US Dollar. Penny is a reference to the one-cent coin. Ben is, you guessed it, a nickname for Benjamin Franklin, whose face appears on the $100 bill in US currency. All three names serve as metaphors for something each of us has a relationship with—*money*.

## MORE THAN MONEY

Ruth, Nick, and Tamara are fictional characters, but they are based on a variety of real-life scenarios I have had with clients, friends, and my own financial journey. Let's revisit the stories of Ruth, Nick, and Tamara now in the context of money.

Ruth is a 40-year-old doctor and mother of two who has a pretty typical relationship with money. She has a six-figure income and loves the life she has built with her family in a beautiful house in the suburbs. She admires, respects, and is perhaps a little in awe of money and what it could enable her to achieve.

But Ruth's financial security has been challenging. She rarely expresses or specifically defines what she wants or needs financially. When her immediate financial needs are met, she goes with the flow and does not think too much about money. She just enjoys her life and trusts that her continued income will be enough for a bright future.

Unfortunately, when faced with financial change or unanticipated financial circumstances, Ruth's income is not as dependable as she expects it to be. When this happens, she becomes concerned about her long-term financial stability. When she hits these rough financial patches, Ruth diligently works to address the issues as best she can, curbing expenses, saving, adjusting, and sometimes lowering her financial goals and expectations for her financial future.

After a while, things usually get back on track, and Ruth feels financially secure again. She feels happy, and her financial expectations begin to grow once more. Unfortunately, Ruth never examines her relationship with money, and therefore she has no idea when, why, or if she will find herself facing financial challenges again. While Ruth's financial rough patches are not ideal, they are also not devastating, so Ruth just accepts what she considers to be the reality of the relationship with money. That is just how it works.

Next door, Nick is not in a healthy relationship with money. He is 52 years old and works as a private school teacher. He married and divorced early in his life and recently remarried. Nick is continually worried about finances and whether he will run out of money. The sad reality is that nothing could be further from the truth, yet that is how Nick feels.

Through his penny-saving behaviors, Nick has amassed a very healthy nest egg and is solidly upper-middle class. He understands that his financial future is secure and that he wants to have a positive relationship with money, but he is hesitant to do so. As a result, he typically ignores his strong financial footing and focuses on working as much as he can as a protective mechanism. Given how much he has, it is remarkable that Nick makes no attempt to comprehend his irrational attitudes toward money and simply believes that things will improve over time.

Meanwhile, Tamara is in a strong and healthy relationship with money. She frequently defines her financial goals and makes necessary plans to achieve them. She takes steps, including certain behaviors such as financial planning, budgeting, saving, and investing, as well as checking her emotions around money, to ensure she will remain financially secure. Like any relationship, Tamara has ups and downs with her finances, but she weathers the ups and downs well through her attention to finances and her emotional preparedness. Her relationship with money is not all work though. She enjoys what her money can do for her life immensely. She also knows money alone is not the only thing that will fulfill her. Having a healthy relationship with money allows Tamara to enjoy her family, valued friends, work, and travel, regardless of her financial wealth, making her feel at peace, respected, purposeful, and truly fulfilled in life. As a result, Tamara is set for a loving, long, and prosperous future.

The truth is that over time, Ruth's income could be sufficient to enable her to become rich, and Nick's savings have also put him on a strong path to becoming rich. But neither Ruth nor Nick live, act, or think this way. Nor are either of them fulfilled. Ruth continues to ride the financial rollercoaster, as I like to call it. She is unlikely to leave her children in debt, but she is also unlikely to leave them any riches and provide them with generational wealth. In an attempt to avoid riding the financial rollercoaster, Nick, on the other hand, continues to act erratically. He will probably continue to worry unnecessarily about his future and work more than he needs to in order to maintain a lower standard of living. Ruth and Nick will have a wide spectrum of emotions in their relationships with money throughout their lifetimes. They look a lot like human relationships!

## DOING THE WORK

Worry, excitement, concern, awe, respect, disappointment, happiness, adjusted expectations, gratefulness—the relationship with money sounds an awful lot like the relationship any one of us might have with another human being. Money is an emotional trigger, the one inanimate object that consistently causes a range of feelings within all of us. Money seems to empower us. We can also feel shame when we do not have enough money, and for some, even shame when we have more money than we need.

For some, money makes us greedy and callous, and for others, jealous and worried. We can feel generous when we help people with our money and then feel guilty when we do not or cannot. Money makes us excited to be able to do something we could not otherwise do. Money triggers in us feelings of security, insecurity, being carefree, and so much more.

Note that I used the words "money makes us" above. That is how we usually think about it, as if money (or lack of money) causes those feelings. It does not. I have asked clients, *If money were no object, what would you be doing right now?* Some of them talk about the expensive things they would buy, but the majority talk about achieving a status of being or feeling an emotion.

I have also asked clients, *What keeps you awake at night?* Again, some discuss financial security, but the vast majority discuss what would make them feel at ease, respected, purposeful, and happy. It sounds a lot like what most of us desire in our interpersonal relationships.

I am not a therapist, but I do know that when people work on their romantic relationships, they have better outcomes. When people hope things will *just work out* in their relationship, it gets a lot riskier. To enjoy a successful romantic relationship, we must not only enjoy the good times, but we also must expect and prepare for problems.

People in successful relationships take responsibility for their part in ensuring the strength of their relationship by having honest conversations about them. They do not expect their partner to be fully responsible for making them feel at peace, respected, purposeful, and fulfilled. They are aware of their own responsibility as well as the challenges they may have in achieving those things. As a result, they proactively work on improving themselves to get there. They do not worry needlessly, but they do the work. They do not seek instant gratification because they know the invest-ment in the relationship is long-term. They quietly go about doing the work, consistently building the best relationship they can.

Yet when it comes to money, so many of us put that relationship on autopilot, simply assuming we will land safely, then become disappointed when we miss the mark. We do this because most of us simply do not know how to do the work needed to build a healthy relationship with money.

## GETTING OFF THE ROLLER COASTER

I have been immersed in a dynamic relationship with money my entire life. As I mentioned earlier, I've spent nearly all of my career working in the financial industry with hundreds of ultra-wealthy clients. Most important, though, is my personal journey through my own relationship with money, having taken more than one ride on the up-and-down financial roller coaster. I will share more details in Chapter 3, but let me paint the big picture for you here.

After growing up comfortably in a wealthy family in New York City, my first experience with the downhill part of the roller coaster came during the year I was a senior in college when the cost of the expansion of our family business nearly jeopardized my parents' ability to pay the tuition and expenses for me to finish my degree. (I am forever thankful that they did.)

Another experience on the roller coaster was getting started with my first job in New York City, only to decide that I needed a law degree to achieve my financial dreams.

So, I went back to school, this time taking out nearly a hundred thousand dollars in loans. Downhill again.

I started back up the hill and got married, had a family, bought a house, and was *living the American Dream*— complete with the typical American debt, including mortgage, student loans, and maxed-out credit cards. I had ridden that roller coaster right into financial insecurity. I knew I needed to be more proactive if I was going to get out of it again, which I did.

Then a divorce happened—which pushed me back into financial insecurity. Down I went. But I had been there before, so I began my usual upward climb of saving and paying down debt to get back to that $0 balance.

On the way up this time, though, I got some real clarity. I could see the pitfalls of riding this rollercoaster of financial stability and instability. I realized I had a good six-figure income, but still did not have any assets or accumulated wealth, and I could very easily be back in debt with a single turn of events. How could this be true when all throughout my career I had been advising and coaching millionaires and billionaires on how to build and protect their wealth.

That is when I began to examine my own relationship with money while studying the habits and learning from the stories of wealthy people, many of whom started out poor. I wanted to know their secret. I obviously knew the financial practices of saving, investing, tax strategies, etc., but those generic financial practices were not what made these people wealthy *and kept them wealthy,* nor was it just their wealth that made them fulfilled. It was not why some of them were Truly Rich.

## TRULY RICH PEOPLE VS. EVERYDAY PEOPLE

Once I leaned in and started paying attention to the stories of financial success and failure of the wealthy, as well as their emotional approach to their wealth, I noticed a distinct difference between the actions and habits of the Truly Rich versus those of what I call Everyday People.

For example, Truly Rich People have an emotionally healthy relationship with money, working at that relationship consistently. They also cultivate and practice specific habits for building, maintaining, and enjoying their wealth. Everyday People tend to not think about their relationship with money nor have purposeful behaviors around their financial management. Everyday People tend to avoid seeking financial advice, while Truly Rich People make it a point to do so regularly. Everyday People often accrue debt without differentiating between good and bad debt, while Truly Rich People understand and leverage the difference.

Over the years, I observed and then defined ten specific and critical habits that Truly Rich People quietly employ and Everyday People overlook. In the pages that follow, I will share The Ten Critical Habits of Truly Rich People and how to begin practicing them. Plus, I will help you avoid the negative behaviors Everyday People often default to instead.

For many years, I was one of those Everyday People. Then I began working on my relationship with money and quietly applying these habits to my own life. When I did that, my entire approach to finances changed, as did the level of fulfillment in my life. With small changes, I was able to secure my financial future while maintaining $0 credit card debt. I gained confidence, had more fun, spent more meaningful time with my family, and enjoyed my personal relationships without constant worry for my financial future.

Rather than just bracing myself for the unknown ups and downs of the financial rollercoaster, I became empowered in my life by changing my relationship with money. As a result, well, I became a millionaire without even noticing it. But I do not define myself as a millionaire, and neither should you. That is an irrelevant status, an artificial goal, and a meaningless term.

What I am is *Truly Rich*.

## CHAPTER TWO

# "MO' MONEY, MO' PROBLEMS"

To become Truly Rich, you may believe all you have to do is make more money. It is a common misconception, but that is all it is. In fact, the opposite can sometimes be true. The more money you make without adjusting your emotional relationship with it, the higher the risk of not preserving your wealth, passing it on, or even enjoying it yourself.

You may have heard the lyric, "Mo money, mo problems" from the popular Notorious B.I.G. song of the same name. While money itself does not cause problems, an unhealthy relationship with money *does* cause problems. To illustrate this, let me share a few fictional stories below that represent different experiences of people I have advised who definitely had what most people would consider "mo' money."

## THE LEGACY CHALLENGE

Brett was a sixty-year-old, jovial man. The first time I met Brett, it was clear he was educated and well-traveled. He was always a delight to spend time with and hear his great stories. Brett's last name was well-known and his heritage impressive. He came from a family that dates back to decorated generals in the Revolutionary War on his father's side and to Spanish nobility on his mother's side. For several years his mother was appointed and served as a US ambassador abroad. His father authored several books on the family's contributions to the war.

Brett and his two siblings had attended prestigious private schools growing up and enjoyed a lifestyle of extravagant wealth. His family owned expensive cars, horses, yachts, and homes. They traveled all over the world. He was well-steeped in the knowledge of the arts and etiquette, trained in fencing, and attended and hosted numerous society events. As a child and young man, Brett was expected to uphold the reputation of the family name and legacy.

Brett had a beautiful wife and two adult sons. They lived in the suburbs of a major metropolitan city in a beautiful stone farmhouse on several acres. Everything in the home was beautifully appointed and decorated, featuring Chippendale furniture and other impressive decor. Brett was very proud not only of the impressive nature of these furnishings, but also of their lineage of family ownership.

He also had a lovely beachfront property at the neighboring shore. However, his most valued property was a castle in Spain. Several years before Brett and I met, he had bought an old castle in Spain connected to his family lineage. After a massive renovation was completed, he and his family began to enjoy summers in Spain at the castle.

As an adult with ample family money, Brett did not pursue a traditional career track. Instead, he became an ambassador of sorts for his family's name and reputation.

The family wealth had been passed down over several generations, mostly in trusts. The income earned in a trust was paid to the current generation, but the principal of the trust was reserved and passed down from generation to generation. Before Brett, his father was the beneficiary of the trust, and before that, his grandfather was the beneficiary. We call this generational wealth. During Brett's father's lifetime, the trust was worth over $100 million, which earned and distributed about $8 million per year to Brett's father.

I served as the trustee of the trust that had been created by Brett's great-grandfather. As trustee, my duty was to protect and preserve the trust principal for all beneficiaries, including future generations. Having worked with families with this kind of generational wealth, I knew how difficult it was to maintain the level of wealth from one generation to the next. With each generation, there are more and more people splitting the same pot of wealth—the trust. Unless different sources of wealth are created by each generation, the trust principal will continue to be diluted as it passes down through the generations.

For instance, when Brett's father passed away, the trust passed to the next generation. But Brett's father had three children. After expenses and taxes were paid, the principal of the trust was divided into separate trusts for Brett and his two siblings. Brett's trust was worth about $25 million, which earned and distributed about $2 million per year to Brett, significantly lower than the $100 million value of his father's trust and $8 million trust income which had fueled their lifestyle.

If you are doing the math in your head, you may have concluded that Brett's $2 million trust income was not enough to support Brett's lifestyle. You are correct. Brett's adult children were not on good footing in terms of generating income either. Brett, keenly aware of this difference, started three new businesses with his sons in the hopes of generating sufficient income for them.

However, these businesses did not generate the income Brett was expecting. In fact, they were losing money. The extravagant cost of Brett's lifestyle was catching up to him as well. Over time, Brett was running short every month on mortgage payments and general living expenses. To the outside world, Brett was living a life of fame and fortune. In reality, he was on the brink of losing most of it.

As the trustee of Brett's trust, I would authorize the trust income payments to Brett as the terms of the trust required, and each quarter I would call him to let him know the date and amount of the income distributed to his account. I was not his personal wealth advisor though, so I was unaware of his overspending with his personal finances. I began to suspect Brett's situation though when he began calling me weeks before a scheduled trust income distribution to seek advances or to request a loan from the trust. Later he began asking me to authorize distributions to him from the principal of the trust in addition to his authorized trust income distributions.

The anxiety in Brett's voice on these calls was palpable. He was scared and frustrated. I had compassion for Brett, but as a trustee, I could not honor his requests because I had a fiduciary obligation to all beneficiaries to preserve the principal of the trust.

Here is the thing though—Brett did not need more money. In addition to the $2 million trust income Brett was receiving every year (and which would continue for his lifetime), Brett had inherited $10 million from his father's personal estate. He could have easily lived on the trust income alone had he not bought and renovated the Spanish castle and other businesses. In addition, he could sell off some assets, like the beach house, or reduce his spending to get out of his current financial situation, but Brett was not interested in doing any of those things, despite how bad things had become. Why?

From our conversations, I gathered that he was using money to feel greater self-worth. Brett was fiercely protective of his family name and proud of the contributions his family had made to freedom and to society over the generations. This was the legacy that each generation before him helped shape. Brett needed to understand how this influenced his relationship with money. I got the sense Brett did not feel as though he was personally contributing to this legacy at that same level as his predecessors, nor were his children. In the end, Brett was neither financially secure nor happy, and certainly not Truly Rich.

## RELUCTANT BILLIONAIRE

May inherited millions from her family. She was always aware that she would receive a lot of money after her father, Tony, died. She had watched her father work very hard his entire life building a successful car part manufacturing business that had employed thousands of people. May had worked in the business under her father for many years.

Tony was a very precise man who retained control over the decisions of the business until he died at the age of 89. It was clear to everyone that he trusted no one with the business. He made most decisions alone and in secret, including the decision to sell the business in the very year he died. Tony explained through his will that despite the incredible success of the business, it had always been a burden and source of frustration to him that he did not want May to have to deal with.

He had relayed that the unexpected offer to buy the business was incredibly lucrative, and he felt it was an opportunity he could not refuse. Tony was thrilled that the proceeds would set May up to do anything she wanted for the rest of her life. But learning after the fact that her father had made an agreement to sell the business without even talking to her, it was clear to May that he had not trusted her to carry on the business successfully. This revelation hurt May deeply.

I was a financial advisor when May was referred to me by Tony's estate attorney. When I started working with her, a trust for her benefit had just been funded with over $1 billion dollars from Tony's estate that would produce over $60 million in income for May per year!

For our first meeting, I had prepared an agenda to go over her goals and plans for how she wanted to manage her new inheritance. I assumed that we would discuss how she might want to use her inheritance to change things in her current financial plan and goals.

But when we sat down and started to review her financial accounts, she began talking about her current expenses and retirement plan. She explained how her current investment income was covering her expenses, leaving a small amount that she was putting into a separate retirement account. She was particularly eager to discuss her concerns over whether the retirement account would be sufficient to meet her retirement needs. I was taken aback by her concern given the significant inheritance she had just received.

When I tried to ease her concerns by bringing up the trust account and the annual income from the trust, she cut me off quickly, saying, "No. That's not my money." I was puzzled, thinking I had misunderstood her concerns. I composed myself and again explained that while she did not own the assets of the trust outright, she was entitled to all of the $60 million annual trust income which would be paid to her directly.

She merely stated that she was aware of the trust's conditions but the money was not hers. After some mild prodding, I discovered that the sale of the business by Tony had shattered May's confidence in her ability to live up to his expectations. How could she possibly manage a billion-dollar trust if she was not able to operate the business? She was well aware that she was the sole beneficiary of the trust but was adamant that she did not want to discuss the income nor the investment management of the principal. She told me to simply invest the money as I assumed Tony would and to add all of the income back to the principal of the trust. I was floored. I had never had this experience with a client.

May's relationship with her inheritance was simply a stand-in for the relationship with her father and their unaddressed issues. May was a bona fide billionaire, but she was not Truly Rich.

## THE UNFORGIVABLE GIVER

Similar outcomes can be seen with wealthy children who have been abused or have experienced trauma with their wealthy parents. I had a somewhat similar situation with a client who had a very dysfunctional relationship with her parents as an adult. She was emotionally distressed and not able to earn a steady living. In fact, she struggled quite a bit.

Her parents were philanthropists who gave millions of dollars to charity every year. Their giving often made the news. The family name was published in many charitable giving reports and bestowed on the wings of numerous institutions.

My client had long stopped spending time with her family and was conflicted when hearing from others about how charitable her parents were. Through her parents' tax strategy planning, my client would receive large distributions of money from her parents every year. Yet she thought of these distributions as a kind of *blood money*. She agonized over taking the distributions, often turning around and giving the money to charity herself.

I cannot begin to understand the difficult and emotional positions nor pass any judgment on the decisions of these individuals. However, it is interesting to note that the money could have helped my client in so many ways. It was the most painful client situation I have experienced and a sad example of not being Truly Rich.

Another example comes not from a client, but from a potential client I decided not to engage. I could see the writing on the wall a mile away. He was another successful entrepreneur who had expectations of his children taking over his business.

However, his children had pursued their own interests and were not involved in the business at all. Although it had been years since his children made those decisions and became involved in their own careers, he remained angry about their decisions.

In his approach to retirement, knowing there was no one who could take over the business, he reluctantly sold it. While the sale was quite profitable, he resented the proceeds because he never wanted to sell. His resentment manifested itself in his relationships with his children. He told me he would require each child to prove they were deserving of any of his money and was seeking my assistance as a trustee to judge and monitor their worthiness.

I declined to work with this potential client who clearly was not Truly Rich.

## A TRULY RICH RELATIONSHIP WITH MONEY

These people all have more money than most people in the world ever will, and yet they are far from being fulfilled. They are rich, but they are not Truly Rich. For each of them, having more money did not move them towards contentment. In each scenario, money seemed to cause them conflict and confusion, leading to inaction or poor choices. The reality, though, is that money does not have the power to cause conflict and confusion, nor to make us act or not act.

According to Investopedia, money is defined as "a generally accepted medium of exchange used to facilitate transactional trade for goods and services." In other words, money is merely an object, a tool, an instrument that possesses no intrinsic qualities or powers. Furthermore, once someone has sufficient wealth to provide for basic needs, there is no correlation between money and happiness or unhappiness.

What can cause conflict and confusion and hold great power over people, though, is *an unhealthy relationship with money.*

An unhealthy relationship with money consists of two elements:

1.  Misguided beliefs about money itself, and
2.  The unconscious substitution of money for unresolved conflicts with *people* or unresolved feelings about *issues.*

The beliefs people may have about money range from viewing money as inherently good, equal to their self-worth, and having the power to solve all problems, to viewing money as inherently bad, causing numerous problems and something to avoid or be secretive about.

The unconscious substitution of money for unresolved conflicts with *people* typically stems from how money was or is used by the people in our lives, particularly our parents and partners. The unconscious substitution of money for unresolved feelings about *issues* typically stems from how we view what we can obtain with money, such as inclusion and acceptance. In other words, money often represents something for us.

These beliefs and unconscious substitutions essentially serve to elevate the abundance or the lack of money for Everyday People to a social status and value which represents either success or failure. When one begins to view money simply as a tool, rather than good versus bad, and understands how money can mask unrelated and unresolved conflicts, an unhealthy relationship with money can become a healthy and positive one. This is the emotional richness, or emotional wealth, that comes with being Truly Rich.

At the same time, when people achieve their best level of financial wealth, they gain additional benefits such as financial security, unique experiences, and the ability to contribute to their communities and help family members achieve goals. This is the financial richness of being Truly Rich.

Once one addresses their relationship with money and achieves emotional wealth, they are poised to develop essential habits to achieve financial wealth. When both emotional wealth and financial wealth are achieved, the true value of money emerges where one can leverage their wealth as a tool towards their success in all areas of their lives, rather than viewing the money as success itself. Their happiness and purpose become aligned with their wealth. In fact, their financial wealth is often a side effect. This is when they become Truly Rich.

## CHAPTER THREE

# WHAT DOES IT MEAN TO BE TRULY RICH?

I was a truly happy child growing up, carefree and loved fiercely by my family. I felt supported by both of my parents to be anything I wanted to be. We had a lot of money during my childhood and adolescent years, but it was not always like that.

We were poor when I was a baby. I recall my father telling me he would look at the inside of my baby shoes to see how deep the toe impressions were to see how long he could hold off before having to buy me a new pair. My parents' parents also had very little, but for my maternal great-grandparents, that was not always so.

My great-grandfather, Elliott Rawlins, was a renowned doctor in Harlem. He and his family lived in a huge house on Astor Row, which for the African-American elite of the 1920s was a powerful symbol of success.

They also owned an income-producing property in the affluent New York Hamptons. But that wealth was lost over the years due to a number of unfortunate circumstances including my great-grandfather's untimely death, the lack of any estate planning by him or my great-grandmother, and archaic property customs for women at the time which stripped ownership of the real estate properties from my great-grandmother in favor of her second husband. By the time Dr. Rawlin's granddaughter—my mother—came along, nothing was left of the wealth her grandfather had built, so she grew up poor.

When my parents started their family, they, too, had very little. I was not aware of this fact though, as by the time I was five, my parents had started a successful business and were experiencing their first taste of wealth. Growing up from that point forward, I knew we had money, but I did not understand what that really meant. I just knew I was happy.

I grew up in New York City and thought I was the luckiest kid in the world because my parents owned a candy store. It was a little storefront on a well-populated corner in West Harlem. Imagine my delight as a ten-year-old walking into the candy store, grabbing a Yoo-Hoo out of the cooler, and getting a kiss from my grandpa (who often worked the register). I would go behind the counter to pick my choice of Sugar Babies, Hershey Bars, rock candy sticks, or a pack of bubble gum candy cigarettes. Yes, I am dating myself, but life was good.

Despite the long hours my parents worked, they were able to spend wonderful quality time with my sister, Karen, and me. As their business became more successful, my parents wanted something bigger. They closed the candy business and opened a true mom-and-pop coffee shop in its place: Perk's Coffee Cup.

Most people knew my father, "Perk" as they called him, from the candy store, but with the expanded clientele in the coffee shop, my father grew in popularity. His infectious personality became a highlight for anyone coming in for a morning plate of pancakes or an afternoon burger. He was exceedingly charming, funny as can be, and good-looking. My mom, Gail, the warmest and most caring person you could ever meet, often referred to him as "Dark Gable."

Soon after opening, the success of the business was readily apparent with people coming not only from the Harlem neighborhood but also from Brooklyn, New Jersey, New Rochelle, and even farther away. Yes, the food was delicious, the place was clean, and it was a good value. But it was my father's presence and my mother's true caring disposition that had people coming in droves.

Perk's Coffee Cup continued an unbelievable stretch of success throughout my elementary, middle, and high school years. With the success came the money, and with the money came my childhood experiences.

We lived large. Birthdays, anniversaries, graduations, Mother's Day, etc. were all occasions to celebrate by going out to lavish restaurants with friends and extended family. It was not unusual for my parents to host large celebration parties at fancy and expensive restaurants. I had my first taste of caviar before I was in high school. Back-to-school and summer clothes shopping meant excursions to Bloomingdales and Nordstroms, leaving with several bags containing thousands of dollars in new fashions.

We vacationed for the month of August every summer in Bermuda in a beautiful house overlooking the ocean. We frequently attended headliner concerts and musicals on Broadway. My sister and I attended dance and gymnastic camps. I went to ski camp in Switzerland. I took piano and violin lessons. I learned to drive in my dad's Mercedes. My parents rented out a popular NYC nightclub for my Sweet 16. My sister and I went to expensive private schools. I even had a driver take me to school every day!

In addition to New York City's affluent, my classroom peers were children of rock stars, actors, dancers, screen-writers, record company moguls, Rockefellers, and even a porn publishing giant. Ben Stiller was actually my classmate before he was famous, and Mick Jagger and then-girlfriend, Jerry Hall, lived next door to the school for a while. It was all normal that celebrities such as Carly Simon, James Taylor, Peter Max, Gregory Hines, and Alfred Uhry were members of the PTA. All were extraordinarily wealthy, much more so than we were. I experienced their Upper West Side apart-ments and vacation homes without understanding the value and what it must have taken to acquire these things. It was all just ordinary to me. I simply assumed that when I grew up, I would live just like them.

As I headed off to college at the prestigious (and very expensive) Ivy League University of Pennsylvania, my parents began a second expansion of the business. They renovated, reinvested, and expanded into a more upscale restaurant and jazz supper club. Not only did people continue to come from near and far, but now noted celebrities and musicians began stopping in and playing sets. We welcomed talent like John Coltrane, Stevie Wonder, and LL Cool J. There were visits from New York Knicks players and New York politicians. Even Robert DeNiro came in one night! It seemed my parents' success and financial security were set in stone. In turn, with my parents' financial wealth as my foundation, my Ivy League education, and all the hobnobbing with the most affluent people in New York City, I was certainly set up for a life of wealth myself.

Then, when I was in my senior year of college, my parents came to me and told me the cost of the expansion of the business had significantly hampered their cash flow and they would not be able to pay for my college tuition that year. I was stunned. For the first time in my life, I felt anxiety about finances. Fortunately for me, they figured it out somehow, and I graduated without any personal debt, for which I am forever grateful. It was then I came to understand that wealth is not an achieved status that is guaranteed forever.

## TAKING THE RIDE

Prior to that time, I had never thought about my parents' financial security, and while they have remained financially independent and secure throughout their lives, that single year when their cash flow wavered was profound for me.

Looking back now, I can see my education and career choices were driven in part by that event. After college, I got a good but low-paying job in advertising in NYC, saved enough over a few years to move out of my parents' home, and then lived on a tight budget. But I was not getting anywhere financially, so I "invested" in more education. I went back to the University of Pennsylvania, this time to law school, in the belief that the credentials and career opportunities of a lawyer would surely prevent the risks of an unstable financial future.

I emerged from law school with a husband and $93,000 in school loans, but I reasoned it was an investment in my career and an insurance policy on my future wealth. It led me to a high-paying law firm job, which I happened to need to begin paying back the school loans.

I became a trust and estate attorney, helping clients with their estate planning and helping families through the difficult dynamics of inheritance after death. I had my first baby, Maya, a couple of years later and scraped up enough savings to put a down payment on a lovely townhouse in an affluent neighborhood in Philadelphia. I figured I had made it to the top. I was living the American dream, and my financial future was bright.

After we had two more children, Alina and Claire, I found myself feeling the need for more balance in my life. Although I was making a very good income, I was working 14 hour days and missing my family. So I did a stay-at-home versus child-care-cost analysis and figured we could afford for me to reduce working to part-time. The move was great for my family, but after a few short years, it took a serious toll on our finances. We adopted some not-so-great financial practices to keep up our lifestyle. As a result, we got into debt using credit cards and the line of credit on our house to pay expenses.

Between this and my school loans, we found ourselves very financially insecure, living paycheck to paycheck with no savings and significant debt. I knew this was not sustainable, so I aggressively started saving again as I did back when

I wanted to move out of my parents' home. Very slowly we began to pay down the debt.

After a few years of this, we were finally back to $0 credit card debt, but I still had significant student loan debt and a big mortgage. I was on the ladder to financial success, but my emotional reserves were becoming depleted. We then experienced a series of scary child care incidents that caused me to stop working completely for a year and take care of my three girls full-time.

Leaving the big law firm life and being at home with my daughters during that time brought a sense of relief for my emotional well-being. Having that time with my family and knowing I was doing the right thing was crystal clear. It was—and is still—the best decision I ever made in my career.

However, it was not long before I not only missed the additional sense of purpose my work gave me, but my family's financial stability was increasingly becoming a concern once again. Money became even tighter, and we were in jeopardy of not being able to keep up on the mortgage. We had sold my car and eliminated all childcare expenses. We did not go on vacations other than the nearby shore with friends. There were no more expenses we could cut. While the work-life balance fed my emotional soul, it was not enough to stave off the financial stress. That is when I started my own law practice to bring in some more income. I was working like a dog again, though, and taking care of the kids, but it put us back on even financial footing.

Then a divorce happened, and the splitting of our assets, including our home. This required me to buy out my ex-husband's share of the tiny amount of equity in our house using borrowed money from a dear friend. The loss of my husband's income, my existing student loans, borrowed money, and now having the full responsibility of the mortgage, pushed me back to financial insecurity. At one point I was at risk of having to sell our home.

I decided to end my law practice and take a full-time corporate role again and began saving and paying down debt to get back to that $0 balance. I could exhale again, but for how long? And how long before my emotional soul would be in jeopardy again?

Meanwhile, my parents were getting older, and it became clear to me that they did not have a plan for their retirement. All those years ago when I decided to go to law school, it had not occurred to me to sit down and definitively tell my parents that I was not interested in running the family business. In fact, I do not think any of us really thought about what would happen to the business. It was such a mainstay in the fabric of our lives that nobody really gave much thought to what would happen to it. It was Perk's. It would just somehow always be there.

So, my parents did not think to sit down and have a conversation with my sister Karen and me either. They just expected to continue to work until one of them became ill or died. Knowing that was not going to work as a realistic plan, my sister, parents, and I came together and had many conversations about what the right next step should be. In the end, my parents sold the business.

As a fully-fledged adult in the sandwich generation, worrying about my financial future, my daughters' future, and my parents' future, I came to understand the financial challenges my parents must have grappled with when I was growing up. As a child, my parents ensured I felt safe, secure, and happy. At the same time, they must have been balancing their relationship with money in the very same way I was now. They were riding that same financial roller coaster with all the thrills, danger, ups, and downs that I was now riding. It seemed that if I could just make enough money, I could get off the roller coaster and be truly happy.

## TO BE TRULY RICH

In my work in the financial industry, I came across many kinds of extraordinarily wealthy families. Some were very happy; some were not all that happy, and some were actually miserable. How could this be? They all had millions and even billions of dollars! If having all the money you could possibly want does not guarantee happiness, and having balance and family connection doesn't guarantee happiness, *then what does?*

As an advisor to wealthy people, I began to see how financial advice, while necessary and important, was only half of the work—and certainly not the most important. While preserving wealth and passing it on to their children was an important goal, being Truly Rich was a much more important life goal of my successful clients and, in many ways, more difficult to achieve. It required serious and committed work. It required being present in all things.

Digging deep into this work with my clients allowed me to see that I was not digging deep into my own life in the same way. It required an introspective and quiet process. I needed to understand my own relationship with money. I needed to look at my past, including the relationship my parents and their parents had with money. I needed to look at my first husband's relationship with money. It never even occurred to me to look at my children's relationship with money, but that became important too.

I also had to be honest with myself and admit that I was not applying the knowledge and wisdom I had shared with and advised my clients on for building strong and healthy relationships with money. I talked the talk, but I was not walking the walk. This long and hard examination was not filled with epiphanies and loud *aha!* declarations. It was consistent, quiet work which, frankly, was uncomfortable at times.

But I started to uncover in more detail what it was that made me happy. Why did I feel so wonderful as a child? I went back to that place in my childhood where I thought my happiness was due to our being *rich*. Was it the money and the things money bought? Was it the house in Bermuda, the clothes, the celebrities, etc…?

No. It was the time spent with my family. It was being with my grandmother, a vibrant and hilarious woman who joined us every August in Bermuda. It was fishing off the shore with my sister while making up songs and stories. It was swimming in the ocean with her. It was my mom teaching us how to play Rummy 500 on the beach and having her undivided attention.

It was not all the summer camps and lessons that made me happy; it was the drive to and from those events while listening to the radio with my mom and eating the bagels she brought us for a snack. It was not driving the Mercedes; it was my dad teaching me to drive. It was not the expensive Madison Square Garden concerts and Broadway performances; it was feeling alive with my family in the middle of a vibrant city.

In other words, it was not the things the money bought. It was a feeling of belonging and experiencing the emotional connection to family and life. Once I was able to connect the dots of these things, I began to see how my behaviors and relationship with money were the real issues.

Money did not create those emotional experiences. My relationships with the people in my family did. My family's wealth, though, had become a substitute for these experiences and relationships. I had been confusing our wealth with our relationships and had assumed a causal relationship between them. I needed to detangle the two.

I was not naïve though. There was a certain level of living I wanted to maintain which required a certain amount of wealth. I needed to focus separately on solutions for establishing and maintaining the necessary practices to steadily accumulate, maintain, and enjoy financial freedom. Once I had detangled what makes me emotionally rich from what makes me financially rich, I could work on them separately.

Now that I had a moment to breathe financially, I could begin to see the pitfalls of riding this rollercoaster of financial stability and instability.

## GETTING OFF THE ROLLER COASTER

What I came to understand and learn from my clients is that they had certain behaviors around finances that are essential to accumulating and passing down generational wealth. Furthermore, these behaviors were habitual. So I began to examine the behaviors and stories of these successfully wealthy people, many of whom started out poor. What was the secret?

I obviously knew the clinical financial practices of saving, investing, and tax strategies, but those generic financial practices were not what made these people wealthy—and kept them wealthy. It was not why they were Truly Rich.

The people who were Truly Rich had financial stability and a secured retirement. These Truly Rich People had healthy relationships and strong communication. They had created generational wealth to pass on to their children and had prepared children who would be good stewards of that wealth. These Truly Rich People had a charitable purpose but also had fun with their good fortune. They had a legacy. But they did not simply luck into these things. They worked at it. Their specific behaviors were consistent among the families and consistently applied within each family. They were in fact, habits. Most importantly, these habits were different from those of Everyday People like me. Over the next several chapters I will share with you The Ten Critical Habits of Truly Rich People I observed and then defined as an insider in the industry.

Once I started paying attention to their stories and their habits, I started applying their lessons to my own life. By making small changes in my behaviors, I was able to build for an early retirement, travel around the world with my family, buy a large and beautiful home, pay for my children's college educations, and generally secure my financial future—with no debt.

More career opportunities opened up for me. I met the perfect man and married him. My husband Gio and I blended our separate families, with me gaining two incredible stepchildren, Chiara and Gio. We became one big amazing family of 7, like a Black and Italian Brady Bunch! My life was so full and rich with relationships, love, fun, security for my now expanded family, and opportunity. I had finally created the right relationship with money bringing all the riches of emotional wealth and financial wealth.

Several years later, this relationship with money and habits was put to the test when I made the choice to leave my then high-paying corporate job. We had just bought our dream home and invested a significant sum of money into the renovations. Our three oldest kids were in college, our youngest would start the following year, and we did not qualify for college financial aid. I did not have another job lined up. But I was not happy. I did not feel valued and felt that my path there was getting smaller. I may have been rich in the financial sense, but I was once again not rich in my emotional life.

Could I really just walk away though? What would happen to the financial wealth I had created? Would my pursuit of emotional happiness derail my financial happiness? But by now I knew the two were not connected. Being unhappy in that job was on account of that specific role at that place and time just not being right for me. The compensation was contributing to my financial richness, but the job was taking away other things that make me emotionally rich. I was more than willing to focus on getting those other things back in balance.

To be Truly Rich is to accumulate both financial wealth and emotional wealth for peace with everything else in your life. Being financially rich simply was not enough. So I left my job. Suddenly, it was not so scary because I knew it was not about the money.

The money had not caused my happiness or unhappiness. It was only money. It was independent of my emotional happiness. I knew that by continuing to work the Ten Habits I had learned, I would be financially secure.

The goal was to make sure I had richness in all parts of my life and remained Truly Rich.

Over the next ten chapters, I will take you through the Ten Critical Habits of Truly Rich People and share how they shaped my journey. The Habits were born out of my observations of wealthy people I have worked with who achieved a level of fulfillment I did not see in *all* wealthy people. The Habits were also shaped by my observations of behaviors of Everyday People, including my own lessons and understanding of behaviors I needed to change in myself.

Each chapter will describe a Habit of Truly Rich People, as well as their specific behaviors behind the Habit, why the Habit is important for building financial wealth, and how it may also impact emotional wealth. Through my own story as well as illustrative character examples, each chapter will also explore the sometimes contrasting behaviors of Everyday People, pitfalls to avoid, and, where relevant, a special note regarding particular vulnerability for women and people of color is included. Most importantly, at the end of each chapter I share practical solutions and advice that Everyday People can use to develop the Habit. Let's get started!

## CHAPTER FOUR

# HABIT 1

## Truly Rich People Are Honest About Their Financial Picture

Truly Rich People make a habit of knowing exactly what their financial picture looks like at all times. On the other hand, Everyday People often are unaware of how good or poor their financial picture is.

The successful clients I have worked with are the ones who can spot a discrepancy in their accounts from across the room. I am talking about people who have millions of dollars and still know if their account summary is off by a few dollars. They can tell you every asset they own and the current market value, as well as how much they just spent on repairs to their house.

They can tell you what they spend on their children. They know exactly what their debt is and when it is due. They know what interest rate they are earning in each of their investment and bank accounts. They know what their mortgage interest rate is as compared to the current rate. They know exactly how much they will need to purchase anything significant and how long it will take to replace the funds for that expenditure.

Taking this a step further, they also know their financial weaknesses and make sure their financial decisions take such weaknesses into account. For instance, if they know they tend to make impulsive buys, they build that into their budget to ensure an impulsive buy does not put them over budget.

Every financial decision they make is made with this knowledge. Truly Rich People are honest with themselves about their financial picture.

Why is this so important? People tend to view the world with either a glass-half-full or glass-half-empty outlook. The way you view the world is typically how you view your finances, but this perspective depends more on personal disposition than facts.

You may believe or desire something to be true, but that does not make it so. If you make financial decisions based on those beliefs and desires rather than on factual data, you can negatively impact your financial security and goals.

A good analogy of this is found in the gambling world. Some people might go into a casino thinking it is their night and dreaming of winning big. They *could* win some and also *could* lose some. That fact does not matter to them. It is the idea that they could win more than they lose that drives them to roll the dice.

However, a factual approach to gambling would tell them they have less than a 50% probability of winning more than they lose. That is what makes it a gamble. When Everyday People do not take a factual approach to their finances, they are essentially gambling with their financial future.

I have observed that Everyday People tend not to know their net worth. Net worth is the total value of everything you own free and clear of any debt.

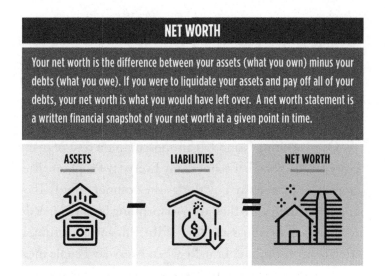

### NET WORTH

Your net worth is the difference between your assets (what you own) minus your debts (what you owe). If you were to liquidate your assets and pay off all of your debts, your net worth is what you would have left over. A net worth statement is a written financial snapshot of your net worth at a given point in time.

|  ASSETS  |  LIABILITIES  |  NET WORTH  |

Knowing your net worth can be scary because you must confront where you are financially versus where you wish to be.

But the only way to get to where you want to be is to make a factual plan for financial growth. When you honestly know your full financial picture, you can begin to see the potential of what your finances can become and create a plan for that financial future.

## PITFALLS TO AVOID

The idea of manifesting what you want in life is quite popular these days. Manifesting simply means that you think and act as if what you wanted was already your reality. There is a lot of research to support using that technique in certain areas of life. However, spending like a rich person to become a rich person is neither a factual nor a good plan. It is easy to confuse drive, passion, and healthy risk-taking with being uninformed of facts.

Winging it each month financially without understanding all the data for the full year and the long-term picture is also a popular practice of Everyday People. Their idea is to just stay out of hot water by keeping on top of expenses and spending what is available. Neither manifesting nor winging it is a great way to approach finances.

Overspending is another all-too-common trait of many Everyday People. That is not to say Everyday People are irresponsible or carelessly buy things they cannot afford. They simply do not realize they are overspending because they do not have a clear understanding of their financial picture. It often happens unintentionally when Everyday People meet their expenses each month, feel they have met their responsibilities, and simply spend the balance of their cash.

However, this end-of-month spending does not take into consideration the risk of assuming either nothing will change with incoming cash flow or unexpected expenses will not pop up. It happens when Everyday People are not tracking their spending or are buying things that require unexpected maintenance. It happens when Everyday People buy things on credit cards that do not require full payment, especially with credit being so easy to get. It happens when Everyday People are simply not saving enough.

Everyday People overspend mostly because they have available cash in their account or credit available to spend.

With credit cards—and now touch pay systems like Apple Pay—making it so easy to make a purchase without even looking at your financial picture, more and more people simply do not have the needed discipline to make an informed decision. If there is cash in the account, or if a purchase goes through, then they think they can afford it and that they are not overspending.

Even some of the millionaires and billionaires I have worked with had this same thinking. Recall Brett and his spending habits? However, the Truly Rich People I worked with—millionaires and non-millionaires alike—always knew how every purchase fit into their overall financial plan.

Another pitfall for Everyday People is to mistakenly think that if they know what they have in their checking account then they know what they can afford to buy. However, knowing how much money you have in your checking account does not equate to knowing your financial picture. Your available cash is not necessarily available for your spending. It is also not necessarily what you *should* spend. What you have in your checking account is not the same as your cash flow. Your cash flow is your available cash from all sources *after* all your current and *future* expenses are paid.

## REAL-WORLD EXAMPLE

Let's break it down with a simple example. Suppose an Everyday Person has a monthly income of $8,000 and monthly fixed expenses of $5,000. That means they have a monthly cash flow of $3,000. They will have $8,000 of cash coming into their account, but they only have $3,000 available to spend each month.

If the fixed monthly expenses are not all deducted from the account on the same day each month (and most bills arrive at different times), they will have cash balances other than $3,000 at various times. For example, they may have a $4,000 balance on a particular day. However, having $4,000 available cash in their checking account does not mean they have $4,000 available to spend. They still only have $3,000 available to spend each month regardless of the balance in their account on a particular day.

All too often, Everyday People spend their available cash because they know that more cash is *probably* on the way next month. But this means they are then playing catch-up next month. And often the month after that. And so on. Overspending like this happens when they do not understand their full financial picture.

Now suppose this Everyday Person also has assets (the value of their house, checking accounts, savings, 401k, etc.) worth $650,000 and liabilities (mortgage, credit card & loan balances, etc.) of $150,000. Thus, their net worth is $500,000. That could be over or under where the Everyday Person thought they were. If it is over, that is great for them and they can keep doing what they are doing. However, if it is under where they thought they were, then they can make a realistic plan for financial growth. Perhaps this Everyday Person wants to build their net worth to $1,000,000 over the next twenty years. They could plan to consistently save and invest half of their $3,000 cash flow which would be $1,500 a month.

When it comes to spending, however, each time this Everyday Person spends more than their monthly cash flow, it will add to the time required to reach that net worth goal.

Because Everyday People are sometimes not honest with themselves about their financial picture, however, they often do not save intentionally and get stuck, never seeming to be able to grow their net worth.

After setting the net worth growth goal in this scenario, Truly Rich People will know they have $1,500 available to spend each month, not the entire $3,000 cash flow, and certainly not the $4,000 checking account balance. Truly Rich People will understand that if they want to make purchases for more than $1,500 in a particular month, it will impact their net worth goal. They understand they will need to spend *less* than $1,500 the next month to stay on track because they fully understand their financial picture and are being honest about their finances.

Before you get the wrong impression, being honest about finances is not always doom and gloom! Quite the opposite. Sometimes when we are honest about all aspects of our financial picture, we discover we actually have room for additional savings, purchases, and ways to reward ourselves.

When I started applying this habit to my own situation, I discovered the market value of my house was higher than I realized. I was not planning to sell my house, but knowing how its value had increased my net worth gave me more confidence about reaching my financial goals.

# ➔ YOUR NEXT MOVE

*Knowing* that Truly Rich People have the habit of being honest about their finances is not the same as *developing* this habit. So, how can Everyday People develop this habit? The simplest way to start is to create a *Personal Financial Statement* (PFS) or a *Net Worth Statement (NWS)*. Just creating a personal financial statement can give you more insight into your financial picture because it requires you to sit down and understand the value of everything that is in your name.

The most important thing is to make sure *everything* is included in your PFS—every asset you own *and* every debt you owe. If you are married or share finances with someone else, then it is critical to include their assets and liabilities in the PFS as well.

A PFS can be very simple or more complex and include things like account details, income, expenses, net worth, investment projections, interest rates, and cash flow. Digital PFSs may allow for direct feeds from your financial accounts. There are dozens of apps and websites available at the time of this writing to help you create a PFS. Your financial institution may also have the ability to help you create one. When I started to apply this habit to my own financial situation, I created my own PFS using a simple Excel spreadsheet. I also used Mint.com, an online interactive app that made keeping my PFS up to date and generally staying on top of things much easier. Find a method that works well for you, because, after all, if you don't use it, it won't help you.

After you have decided on the format and vehicle to create your personal financial statement, the next step is to use it regularly. Do not simply create a PFS and tuck it away, never to be seen again. Truly Rich People use tools like this in the same way Everyday People might use newspapers, a weather app, or a GPS while driving. We use these tools to keep us informed, make sure we are prepared, and tell us where we are going. The PFS is no different. Relying on old news, weather from several months ago, and outdated GPS directions would not be helpful. In fact, it could be dangerous! Simply taking a single snapshot of your finances at one point in time—and then relying on that information going forward without continuing to update and review it—is also not helpful and is financially dangerous. Truly Rich People update their PFS at least quarterly.

Before I created my own PFS, I was pretty much in the dark about my financial picture. When it came to paying bills, I would toss them in a pile when they arrived and wait until *bill day* to address them. The bills made me feel anxious. I would wait until they had reached critical mass, and then I would sit down in front of my checkbook and pay them all at once. With only one eye open, not really wanting to see my financial reality, I would balance the checkbook and see what was left. I would then put it all away and not look at it again until the next cycle.

Once I started applying the Truly Rich Habit of being honest about my financial picture, I was amazed at how it made me feel. When I first created my PFS, I became obsessed with it. Each time I received a statement for an account or made a significant expenditure, I would imme-diately update my PFS. The PFS—and more importantly, the honesty—empowered me with regard to my finances rather than scared me. I felt ready to tackle any financial challenge, good or bad. Each time a new bill arrived in the mail, I opened it immediately so I could see the impact it would have on my PFS. I would pay it, and then update the account I paid it from with the new balance. In short, I felt in control rather than anxious.

By actively and consistently using my PFS, I ended the cycle of not knowing the reality of my financial picture. From that day forward, I chose to always be honest about my financial picture and was on my way to becoming Truly Rich.

## CHAPTER FIVE

# HABIT 2

## Truly Rich People Live Within Their Means

*L* *ive within your means.* It is a saying that has been around for many years. But what does it really mean? Living within your means sounds like simply buying only what you can afford. However, as we saw in the last chapter, spending and spending habits take on different meanings for different people.

Often Everyday People see wealthy people spending large sums of money—expensive vacations, beautiful homes, lots of big-ticket toys—living the life of luxury that perhaps they themselves would like to live. It is true that with significant wealth and cash flow often comes a particular *high-life* lifestyle that is visible to everyone. It is no wonder so many Everyday People think that if they just had a lot of money they could spend freely on whatever they please and not have to worry about anything else.

Here is a little piece of advice: Do not let how other people live and spend their money fool you. There is a difference between spending *a lot of money* to live a life of luxury versus spending *what is affordable for you* within your specific financial picture. What is affordable for you *may* be a life of luxury, but it may not.

On the other hand, there are many financially rich people who live a luxurious lifestyle but end up not able to sustain it. One area where this happens very often is when people acquire wealth suddenly, as is the case with lottery winners and some musicians, athletes, and other celebrities. Perhaps such financially rich people did not come from wealth and suddenly find themselves having a lot of money and significant cash flow. Unfortunately for these sudden millionaires, the habit of living within their means does not magically appear along with the infusion of money. In many of these situations, the opposite effect happens, and they begin to spend and behave in ways completely out of character and beyond their means.

In my profession, it is not uncommon for financial advisors to steer clear of sudden millionaires as clients. It is quite challenging to advise clients with money when they lack the discipline to live within their means. All you have to do is Google "lottery winners who lose it all" to see just how easy it is to spend through what seems like all the money someone could ever need.

When Truly Rich People—millionaires or not— are honest about their financial picture (as we saw in the previous chapter) and have their PFS mapped out showing exactly what they can afford within their financial plan, they then stick to that plan by living within their means.

They understand their cash flow and the boundaries of their wealth; therefore, they know exactly what they can afford. In turn, the amount of their net worth and cash flow within their financial plan dictates the lifestyle they can live. They understand that going beyond what they can afford will impact their financial future, so they adjust their lifestyle accordingly. They know the only thing worse than not having what you want now is having less than what you already had later.

I have worked with clients who can afford to buy exceedingly costly things, such as their own airplanes or yachts, and yet choose not to because of the impact such a large expenditure would have on their overall financial plan and goals. They have made the disciplined decision to forego something they *can* afford because of the potential long-term impact it would have on their financial plan.

That does not mean another family who can afford to and does purchase a yacht is not living within their means *if* it fits within their financial plan. It all comes down to what your specific financial picture dictates. It also comes down to personal choice. One person may look at their financial situation and decide that eating out at restaurants every night is important to them because they do not like to cook. They may adjust other spending areas to allow for higher restaurant spending. Giving themselves this luxury within the structure of their financial discipline is what being Truly Rich looks like. It is taking the honesty from Habit #1 and applying it with the discipline of Habit #2 to live within your means.

# ⊙ YOUR NEXT MOVE

Knowing that Truly Rich People have the habit of living within their means is not the same as developing this habit yourself. So how can Everyday People develop this habit? We saw in Chapter 4 how not knowing your cash flow can lead to overspending. But there is more to it than simply knowing your cash flow. It is planning for how the cash flow is spent and then having the discipline to stick to the plan. It is about creating—and sticking to!—a budget.

We learned in the last chapter that your cash flow is your available cash from all sources *after* all your expenses are paid. A budget is simply a spending plan for your cash flow for a specific period. The most important aspect of creating a budget is accurately understanding and documenting your expenses. This is where many Everyday People go wrong. If Everyday People just wing it, as we previously discussed, or if they do not document all expenses, then the budget will not be accurate. They end up violating Habit #1 by not being honest with themselves.

The first thing to understand about expenses is that they are not just bills. Your expenses include everything you spend money on. The good news is that expenses—and therefore your budget—can be adjustable to a certain extent. While you may not be able to immediately adjust the amount of some expenses, such as rent or utilities, you *can* adjust other expenses, such as food and entertainment. The most important thing is to get an accurate picture of what you are currently spending.

| MAY SPENDING PLAN: | Income: | $4000 |
|---|---|---|
| | Total budgeted: | $3960 |
| **Student Loans** | Hers: | $300 |
| Total: $500 | His: | $200 |
| **Living** | Rent: | $700 |
| Total: $900 | Internet: | $70 |
| | Electric: | $30 |
| | Cell phones: | $100 |
| **Food** | Groceries: | $200 |
| Total: $400 | Restaurants: | $200 |
| **Insurance** | Life: | $25 |
| Total: $95 | Renters/car: | $70 |
| **Amusement** | Hers: | $100 |
| Total: $220 | His: | $100 |
| | Netflix: | $20 |
| **Car** | Gas: | $300 |
| Total: $325 | Oil: | $25 |
| **Clothing** | Laundry: | $20 |
| Total: $220 | New: | $200 |
| **Needs** | Debt snowball: | $500 |
| Total: $800 | Home care: | $100 |
| | Tithe: | $200 |
| | Savings: | $500 |

When I first applied this habit of living within my means, I began by saving the receipts for every penny I spent for a full three months. During that time, I did not alter my normal spending because I was employing Habit #1 and was being honest with myself about my true spending. I needed to see how I normally spent in order to see what my true expenses were. I call this a *cash flow analysis,* or in other words, *Where is all my cash going?*

Reviewing and analyzing every expense—whether it is fifty cents, fifty dollars, or five-hundred dollars—is incredibly illuminating. I was shocked to see how much money I was spending at Rite Aid every week! My children were babies at that time, so I expected to have a lot of drugstore needs such as diapers. But when I started to review the individual receipts, I saw a pattern of impulse buying. Drug stores are no longer just pharmacies. It is amazing what you can find there and buy on impulse!

Just as creating a PFS empowered me rather than scared me, so did my new understanding of my spending habits and ultimately my expenses. The next thing I did was to create a Rite Aid budget within my overall budget. I made a list of all the things I went to Rite Aid for that were legitimate need-based expenses and limited my spending to only those things. That meant that if I saw a lovely three-wick candle on sale for $10 while I was in Rite Aid, I just said no to buying it because it was not in the budget. Small impulse buys may not be noticeable to Everyday People in the moment; however, when we have a clear budget and recognize and proactively remove impulse buys from our spending, the impact on reducing expenses can be significant.

After doing my cash flow analysis, the next step was to determine how I would spend my available cash flow, what I could afford after my expenses were paid. This is where size matters. The size of your cash flow can determine how strictly you need to budget. Generally, the smaller your cash flow, the more strict your budget should be because there is less room for error. However, the larger your cash flow, the more detailed your budget categories should be because it can be easier to lose track of smaller expenditures. Once again, it is about being honest with yourself. If your cash flow is small, it may not be practical to budget too strictly when emergencies and other needs arise, but it is important to know what your cash flow is and not to overspend.

## NEXT-LEVEL HONESTY

To continue being honest with myself as I applied Habit #2 and lived within my means, I decided to continue to track my cash flow spending beyond the original three-month cash flow analysis. I knew how easy it would be for me to make an impulse buy here and there, and I was worried I would do so even with my newfound discipline. I wanted to be able to truly evaluate my spending on a regular basis and not wonder what happened at the end of the month if I was somehow off-budget.

In addition to creating a budget, I began to use a single credit card for all my spending.

**Interest Rates:** One of the most important features of a credit card is the interest rate. It affects the cost of carrying a balance on your credit card, a cost you want to avoid or minimize. The credit card rate (APR or annual percentage rate) is listed in the credit card disclosure. The more you understand your credit card interest rate, the better you can use your card to your advantage and save money on interest in the long run.

**Perks:** Using miles and points to book award flights and upgrades using credit card rewards is easier than you would think. For instance, I have leveraged my credit card usage to pay for family vacations entirely with my credit card points. I have millions of points because I have exclusively used one credit card for all my spending for over a decade. But be sure to keep your balance to a minimum, as interest rates and fees on balances will far outweigh the benefits you receive with points.

I closed all other credit cards, including store charge account cards (yes, I had way too many of those). I only used cash if I absolutely had to, and I gave myself a weekly cash allowance. As a result, when my credit card statement arrived, I was able to track all my spending to see how I was doing.

Taking it a step further, I then opened separate bank accounts for different purposes (some banks have a nice feature where you can open one account but provide segregated buckets within the account for budgeting things such as reserve, spending, and growth). I had my main checking account into which my income was deposited and from which all my budgeted expenses were made. Then I had a separate account for savings. Yes, within my budget, I had an expense that was strictly for savings because part of my larger financial plan was growing my net worth. I had a third account for accumulating college funds. Finally, I had a fourth account for a travel fund, because it was important to me to have short-term personal goals to reward me for my discipline.

Each month I made direct transfers from my checking account in specifically budgeted amounts to each of the other accounts. The next step was to set up automatic bill pay through my online banking for all my known fixed expenses. When all was said and done, I had funds automatically going in and out of my accounts according to my budget.

Over the years, these amounts, accounts, and purposes changed. For instance, as my children got older, I opened separate bank accounts for each of them. Each child had an allowance amount allocated in my budget which was automatically transferred into each of their respective bank accounts. Still today, I keep a budget, separate accounts, automatic transfers, and automatic bill payments. This was my personal method, but there are many creative ways to budget and stick to it if you are creative and put your mind to it.

By creating a budget and having the discipline to stick to it, I was able to live within my means, but I was also beginning to shift my relationship with money. When my budget did not allow for me to spend on the things I previously thought were necessary to create the experiences that gave me that feeling of belonging and the emotional connection to family (vacations, fancy celebrations, private schools, etc.), I was forced to come up with other ways to create experiences that evoked the same feeling and connection.

Some of these changes were significant, such as sending my children to public and charter schools rather than private schools and giving up our car to opt for a car share program. Both decisions led us to invaluable experiences though: a Spanish language immersion program providing my children with the ability to be bilingual, and me riding a bike again for the first time in years to get around town. Other changes were small but emotionally impactful, such as taking staycations and creating our so-called celebration box filled with streamers, costumes, favorite recipes, cake decorations, and more, and which my girls excitedly scrambled to pull out for family celebrations in place of going out to restaurants.

The most unexpected and rewarding experience that came out of curbing my unchecked cash flow spending occurred during the summer my girls were all under the age of seven, when most of their friends were attending private summer day camps. To create enriching experiences similar to their peers', I structured our weekdays just like camp, with field trips, arts and crafts projects, putting on plays, special camp snacks, and much-needed daily nap time so I could work! I gave them official camp t-shirts and told them they were going to "Camp Mali MAC," an acronym for Mali (the country we decided to learn about that summer) and each of their initials (Maya, Alina, and Claire). They loved Camp Mali MAC so much! Imagine my surprise when one day a neighborhood parent asked me for information about Camp Mali MAC for her daughter, assuming it was a real camp based on hearing how my girls spoke about their experiences. That summer, I began to see how being financially rich was quite different from being Truly Rich.

Thus far in this chapter, I have been addressing Everyday People using a budget to avoid overspending so as to live within their means. But what about those Everyday People who are truly just trying to make ends meet? When you are barely getting by, it may seem futile to have a budget because everything you spend is necessary. In fact, it may seem there is never enough money for all the things you truly need to get by. Similarly, people who find themselves with significant debt might not think a budget is important because all their cash flow must go towards their debt.

Even in these situations, however, I highly recommend implementing the lessons from Habits #1 and #2 by creating a PFS, doing a cash flow analysis, and creating a budget. This will allow you to begin to plan your financial freedom. It all starts with identifying your goals and then making a plan to achieve those goals. For instance, if the issue at hand is insufficient income to meet necessary expenses, a PFS, a cash flow analysis, and a budget will show you your income gap and help you to seek specific job opportunities and additional sources of income to bridge the gap.

If debt reduction is a goal, these habits and tools will allow you to map out which expenses you may be able to cut and for how long you need to divert that same amount to paying down the debt until the debt is reduced. I call this a *debt reduction budget* where you steadily begin to dig yourself out of debt. Your debt reduction budget does not have to be a permanent budget; it can be just for the period of time necessary to reduce your debt to the level you are comfortable with to then begin diverting some of it towards a different goal or resume the original expense. I created and followed a debt reduction budget for my student loans and credit card debt, which I describe more fully in Chapter 6.

## CHAPTER SIX

# HABIT 3

## Truly Rich People Leverage Credit but Manage Debt

T ruly Rich People strategically leverage credit but manage debt. On the other hand, Everyday People loathe but also often end up misusing both.

Wealthy people can and do borrow significant sums of money. For decades, I have had an insider's view and understanding of how wealthy people use the bank lending and credit process to obtain significant loans, lines of credit, and other financing for their businesses and personal ventures.

I have observed wealthy people make major property acquisitions and improvements; invest in real estate, lucrative private equity funds, and other assets; grow their businesses; and achieve other personal goals, all with borrowed money. Most lawyers and other professionals who become partners and principals in profitable partnerships—thereby increasing their income and building generational wealth—do so with partnership financing. In some very sophisticated situations, wealthy people even save taxes by borrowing money! In fact, I cannot think of one wealthy client I have worked with that did not borrow money and carry some type of debt.

At the same time, Truly Rich People are careful to set their borrowing to a specifically designed amount. They diligently pay down their debt balances to keep within that amount, and they will even use loans with better terms to pay off other loans with inferior terms. As you might expect, they must always be aware of their total outstanding debt to do so. (See Habit #1!)

In contrast, Everyday People can seem a bit confused. They often try to steer clear of *all* debt. Some do this because they have had bad experiences with debt and never want to go through it again. Others believe borrowing money only benefits banks. Still others believe borrowing makes one poor, so it is better to always pay for things outright.

However, some Everyday People also find their credit card limits and home equity lines to be irresistible. They use that borrowed money as a means for obtaining the things they want without much thought. As a result, Everyday People who try to avoid debt still may end up with more of it than they would like.

People borrow money and incur debt for numerous reasons, good and bad, necessary, and not. Whatever the reason, the greatest risk Everyday People face when they incur debt is falling into a debt cycle. This happens when a person uses a loan, credit card, or other kinds of financing to obtain something they do not have the cash flow to obtain. Inevitably, the ability to pay off that debt in a timely manner fails.

As unpaid interest and penalties on the original debt begin to grow, incurring new debt is the only way to pay it off. But the amount of the new debt must be enough to cover the old debt *plus* the unpaid interest and penalties on the original debt, which makes the new debt even larger than the original debt. Since the ability to pay off the original debt failed, it follows that the ability to pay off the new debt will also fail. Interest and penalties on the new debt then begin to grow and the cycle starts all over. It is easy to see how Everyday People loathe debt but still overuse credit.

Here is a simple example of this:

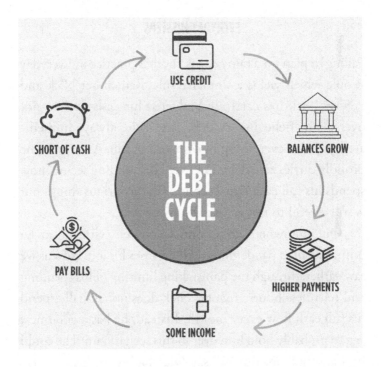

Recall the characters, Ruth and Buck, from earlier. Ruth has no debt, but she and her husband also tend to live beyond their means using credit cards to pay for things they do not have the cash flow to purchase each month. Their family had a challenging financial year, but Ruth wants to give the family a great experience and opportunity to be together. They decide to take a trip over the winter holidays.

Not having saved or budgeted for this trip, they decide to max out the credit cards and are willing to pay it all down over time. Not knowing their full financial picture, Ruth is unaware of how much of a stretch the higher credit card payments will be. A few months after they get back from the vacation, they begin to fall into the debt cycle.

## EVERYDAY MISSTEPS

Failing to plan for a rainy day is another practice of Everyday People which yields a similar result. Remember Nick and Penny? Nick has carefully budgeted his cash flow to not overspend. Believing all debt is evil, he always immediately pays for everything in cash and in full. As a result, he proudly carries zero debt. Let's say Nick, feeling secure, now spends his full cash flow each month on various things but is still careful to not go over budget.

Out of nowhere, an unforeseen and rare virus causes an unprecedented pandemic, and Nick loses his job. Now as we saw earlier, through the painstaking limiting of his spending and relentless hours at work, Nick does not actually spend his full cash flow every month. Instead, he has a good nest egg to probably hold him over in this scenario until he could find another job. But let's say Nick had spent his full cash flow every month and therefore did not have a good nest egg to fall back on, like so many Everyday People. The problem then becomes that although they have no debt, they also do not have enough savings. This is likely due to their cash flow budget not including an allocation of savings which would increase the amount of their assets and net worth for a rainy day/emergency fund, such as a pandemic.

Without available cash flow to address the emergency, they need to take out a loan to cover their lack of income. Eventually, they too fall into the debt cycle. Sometimes, it is even worse when an Everyday Person has never borrowed and cannot even obtain the credit needed to cover the emergency, having to sometimes turn to detrimental lending with exorbitant fees and interest rates.

It is important to take special note of cultural differences regarding the vulnerability of getting into a debt cycle. As discussed in the Appendix, while this behavior is shared across all types of Everyday People, white people often may be able to avoid the debt cycle in ways black people may cannot. As an example, statistically white people have access to more favorable terms on traditional loans, family loans at little or no interest, or even receive gifts from relatives, including inheritances, which can entirely provide for their emergency fund.

As you will find illustrated in the Appendix, black people, and black women particularly, rarely receive inheritances nor do they have family members who are able to help them financially. Furthermore, if black people are able to secure traditional lending, it is typically more costly for them than their white counterparts. But far more often they are denied for traditional lending, leading to reliance on credit cards and other detrimental lending with even more costly terms.

For black women, the stats are even more grave.

Truly Rich People get into a habit of a very different kind. Truly Rich People understand the risk of carrying high levels of debt, but they also understand the advantages of borrowing. Let's consider Tamara. Rather than using all her cash flow or other available funds to pay for everything, she strategically uses attractively structured credit to do so. She then uses a small portion of her cash flow to manage this new debt. Good debt management is the critical part of this habit. On-time payments, keeping debt to credit ratios in line, paying down balances, etc. are the key. This provides Truly Rich People the ability to make large purchases when they need to, preserve their cash flow, and adhere to their budget.

There is an additional advantage most Everyday People do not know about when it comes to managing debt. Good debt management provides Truly Rich People with future opportunities to borrow again (leverage credit) because this positive debt management cycle establishes strong credit for them. This is why Truly Rich People can—and do—borrow significant sums of money. They have learned how debt and credit go hand in hand and are not afraid to use them together. They are in the driver's seat regarding debt, not the other way around. It is how Truly Rich People grow and preserve wealth.

# ⊜ YOUR NEXT MOVE

So how can Everyday People develop the habit of strategically leveraging credit but managing debt? It begins with education. So many Everyday People are under the impression that people who have millions of dollars do not need to borrow money. In Chapter 5, I described how Everyday People who see others living a life of luxury might believe such people can spend what they want without thinking and do not have to budget. But we saw that Truly Rich People do budget in order to live within their specific means.

Everyday People who understand this still might conclude that the budget and cash flow of Truly Rich People simply must be large enough to pay for everything Truly Rich People have or want. But as you can see, Truly Rich People do borrow money. In practicing the other critical Habits #1 and #2 (being honest and living within their means), Truly Rich People do the work to educate themselves about debt and credit in ways that can enhance their financial picture.

Before I understood the power of leveraging credit and managing debt, I fell into many of the Everyday People practices. As I shared earlier, my significant law school loan debt contributed to my financial roller coaster ride: I could not afford to pay for law school on my own; I did not have the cash flow. So, I borrowed money to pay for it instead.

> Interesting fact—Black women owe 22% more in student debt than white women according to a new report from The American Association of University Women.

While I knew that I clearly did not have $100,000 to repay the loan upon graduation, I believed a lawyer's income would be sufficient to pay down the debt in a somewhat short period of time. After I graduated, I started working as a lawyer and began making a lot of money.

However, the interest and principal payments on the loans were so high that I had to use most of my income (cash flow) to make the payments. As a result, I had very little cash flow left over. I never made the time to budget because I was a young lawyer working insane hours, and I believed my income would only rise over the years so I could budget later.

Instead, to address my insufficient cash flow I used the credit cards I easily obtained to pay for dinners at the end of the long weeks, for expensive suits I needed to look my best in the office, and for much-needed vacations. My income did rise each year, but it still was not enough to cover the gap, so I continued to use credit cards for the difference.

After my first child, Maya, was born, I decided to return to work on a part-time basis so I could spend the time with her that I felt was important. It was the best decision I could have made for my family, but it also had a huge impact on my income. As a result, I got further into the debt cycle and it became more and more difficult to dig out of it.

I could not believe that despite having grown up with wealth, obtaining two Ivy League degrees, becoming a lawyer, working for a prestigious law firm on partnership track, and making a significant amount of money, I could not get out of this cycle of debt. I felt foolish for borrowing such a large amount of money and was embarrassed that I had not become a successful enough lawyer to pay it all off. I felt like a failure and blamed the evils of loans and credit cards for my predicament. I had overused credit, and I loathed the debt. I vowed, *If I could ever get out of this debt cycle, I would never take out another loan or use a credit card again....*

Fortunately, I did not stick to that plan. After working on my relationship with money, I began to understand that debt was not evil. It was simply a tool that I had leveraged to accomplish a pretty amazing thing—my law degree. It was my other behaviors of not budgeting, overspending, and not managing my debt that created the debt cycle I was in. This new way of thinking about money, including debt, further shifted my relationship with money and motivated me to get in the driver's seat. I could not turn back time and make the debt disappear, but I did have the power to make changes in my behaviors to reduce it.

## PLAN OF ATTACK

The first thing I did was employ Habit #1 and Habit #2. Creating a personal financial statement and knowing my net worth gave me confidence about reaching my now clearly defined financial goals. I also started educating myself about debt and credit. I stopped beating myself (and my money) up over the existing debt, started cutting expenses, and started a system-based debt reduction plan to eliminate my school loans and credit card debt. I did this by creating a budget with a prominent line for making consistent debt reduction payments over and above what I was currently paying towards my debt, which was merely the minimum payments due.

Another important key to my debt reduction plan was keeping a close eye on bank interest rates on loans and deposits. As soon as home mortgage interest rates dropped below my original home mortgage interest rate, I refinanced my mortgage and used the extra monthly savings towards increasing the amount of my budgeted payments in my debt reduction plan.

From the education I did on debt and credit, I had learned that school loans were not as beneficial as home loans. This is because the typical home mortgage can be refinanced, allowing for a decrease in the interest rate given at the beginning of the loan term to a lower current rate. Federal school loans typically cannot be refinanced and carry the same fixed interest rate from the beginning of the term to the end.

Additionally, home loans are secured by an asset, your home, which has the ability to increase in value. The amount owed on your home as compared to this increase in value is called a loan-to-equity or loan-to-value (LTV) ratio. It is what allows you to obtain a line of credit over and above your outstanding mortgage balance. School loans are unsecured, and therefore there is no LTV. They simply must be paid in full. Educating myself about debt and credit showed me there was a difference in the quality of certain types of debt—*good* debt and *bad* debt.

My school loans were obtained in a high-interest rate period, and therefore had a higher interest rate than the refinanced home mortgage rate. So when the time was right and rates dropped further, I refinanced my home mortgage again. Only this time, because I knew my exact net worth, which included the increased available equity in my home, I knew I would be able to obtain a home equity line of credit (LOC) along with the refinancing. I then leveraged credit—my new LOC—to pay off the entire balance of my higher interest rate school loans. Furthermore, due to the much lower interest rate I was now paying on the LOC balance in place of the higher student loan interest rate, I once again was able to put these additional monthly savings towards increasing the amount of my budgeted payments in my debt reduction plan for a second time. Equally important, I eliminated bad debt (the school loans) and replaced it with good debt (home mortgage).

Here is the bottom line: After the second refinancing and obtaining the LOC to pay off my entire school loan debt balance, my new outstanding combined mortgage and LOC balances were exactly the same as my prior outstanding combined mortgage and school loan balances before the transaction. Think about that; I did not take on more debt, my income and external inflows of cash flow had not changed, and I did not change any other spending in my budget. Yet, by leveraging credit (the refinancing and LOC), I was able to *triple* the amount of my original payments going to my debt reduction plan. All by just watching interest rates and understanding the different kinds of debt I had. Everyday People typically do not have a strategy about how they incur nor pay down debt.

> It is important to take special note of cultural differences regarding attitudes towards home mortgages. As illustrated in the Appendix, many black people have cultural experiences with homeownership that differ greatly from their white counterparts. As a result, many black people tend to pay down good debt such as home mortgages over bad debt such as credit card balances because they feel better about putting money towards "securing" their home.

As I mentioned in Chapter 4, I began to use a single credit card for all my spending to hold myself accountable for tracking my spending. But this had an important secondary purpose. As I continued to learn about debt and credit, I understood how certain behaviors and events impact one's credit. The obvious impacts were making payments on time and obtaining a high amount of available credit.

But there were other impacts—such as how much of that credit you use and inquiries from creditors—which I was not aware of, including some that seemed to fly in the face of what many Everyday People believe. For instance, using your credit, having a high amount of available credit, and holding a very long credit line all demonstrate responsibility and good standing with creditors and have a positive impact on your credit score.

However, having too many credit lines poses a risk for creditors that you might use all of your available credit at once, thereby increasing your outstanding debt to a level that may be hard for you to repay, and this has a negative impact on your credit score. When I closed all my credit cards except one and started using that one card consistently for all spending, it significantly boosted my credit over time. However, I continued to manage my debt, and as part of a system-based debt reduction plan, I was disciplined in not using any of that increased credit for unplanned spending and stuck to my budget.

Understanding how credit and debt works is not always easy or intuitive. However, there are numerous articles, books, websites, and more that are easy to understand. In addition, later in Chapter 10, I will show you how you can gain access to financial secrets, tips, and advice, which can often involve access to credit and funding sources not easily available and which most Everyday People never hear about.

As I continued to reduce my credit card debt, eventually to zero, I continued to use my one credit card in this way, paying off the entire balance (bad debt) each month. Continuing this habit even today, I have enjoyed watching my credit score increase to the top of the range and my access to credit soar into the seven-figure level over this period.

I have always kept a home mortgage (good debt), and although I have the means today to pay my current mortgage off in full, I strategically do not pay down this good debt other than through regular monthly mortgage payments. Leveraging credit is how I obtained a larger home, maximized my investment earnings, purchased investment real estate, and so much more. Debt and credit education made me savvy and strategic about money and might be one of the most important habits that shaped my current relationship with money and made me Truly Rich.

## CHAPTER SEVEN

# HABIT 4

## Truly Rich People Invest

Truly Rich People invest. Everyday People do not invest, or simply do not invest enough.

Investing has been the foundation for my entire career in the financial services industry. Without exception, every wealthy person I have ever advised invests. How wealthy people invest varies greatly and could take up volumes to describe and discuss. This book is neither a primer on investing, nor does it provide investment secrets, stock tips, nor any other investment advice. Make no mistake, though—to be Truly Rich, one *must* invest.

Why is investing so important? It comes down to simple math: *Compound Interest* and *Return on Investment.* Return on investment (ROI) is the measure of how much financial benefit (such as interest) you receive from an investment. Investment interest is the money you earn as a result of an increase in the value of your principal investment.

Compound interest occurs as a result of accumulating and reinvesting such earned interest, rather than cashing it out. As a result, interest earned in the next period is earned on the principal investment *plus* the accumulated and reinvested interest. In other words, it is interest *on* interest. The greater the ROI, the greater the compound interest.

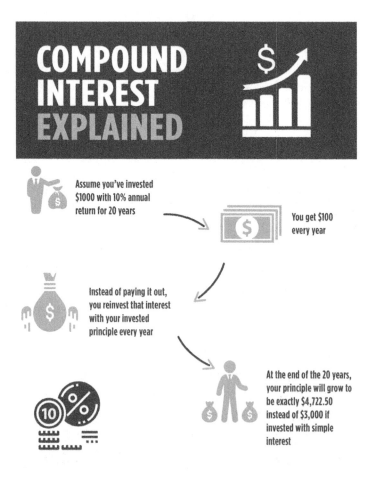

Compound interest and ROI apply to all the ways people use their money, including simply saving. For instance, saving $10,000 in a traditional deposit savings account today will earn annual interest of about .03% or $3.00. If over a period of three years at that same rate with no additional deposits, you take the $3.00 in interest out of the account each year, you would have earned $9.00 in interest (your ROI) on the original $10,000 after three years. If you did not take out the interest, at the end of the three years the compound interest would increase the ROI from $9 to $10. A dollar is certainly not a big deal.

But that's a simple example. Let's consider the same $10,000 savings in a better interest-bearing account, such as a CD earning 3% or $300 in annual interest. If you take the $300 in interest out each year, you would earn $900 in interest (your ROI) on the original $10,000 at the end of the three years. If you did not take out the interest, at the end of the three years, the compound interest would increase the ROI from $900 to $928. Still not a big deal.

Over time, though, say a period of thirty years, that ROI on the original $10,000 would be $9,000 ($300 x 30 years) if you kept taking it out as compared to $14,273 if you left it in and leveraged compound interest, so the total value of the account would be $24,273. Still, a $5,273 difference is perhaps not a big deal for some.

But now let's look at how the combination of compound interest, time, *and* additional contributions has a dramatic impact. For instance, if you contributed an additional $5,000 to the original $10,000 each year, at the end of the 30-year period your original principal investment would be $160,000 ($5,000 x 30 years + $10,000), but your ROI with compounded interest would now be $109,287, and the total value of the account would be $269,287, as compared to $24,273.

However, interest rates for even the best interest-bearing accounts are very low compared to average ROI on stock market investments. If you invested the same original $10,000 plus the additional $5,000 contributions each year in the stock market, earning an average interest rate of 6%, with compound interest the total value of the account would be $476,444 at the end of the same 30-year period. Compared to the CD example, that is an additional $207,157 in interest benefit for the same initial $160,000 principal investment and 30 year time period.

In these examples, saving $10,000 in a traditional bank account for 30 years and spending the yearly interest each year gives you a total ROI of $14,273. Investing the same $10,000 in the stock market and adding just $5,000 each year rather than spending the yearly interest gives you a total ROI of $207,157. Now that *is* a big deal. This is why budgeting and saving pay off.

As you can see, investing typically grows wealth at a much greater ROI than simply saving. Truly Rich People invest to build wealth in a shorter period of time.

Why is it, then, that Everyday People do not invest or do not invest enough? Everyday People can find investing to be risky as well as intimidating. They work hard to earn their money, and they often mistrust putting their money in vehicles they may not fully understand.

For some, it stems from a mistrust of the stock market or of investment professionals. Others are simply afraid of losing their money or not having immediate access to it.

Some Everyday People believe investing is just too complicated, while others may want to invest but believe they lack the financial resources to do so. Savings accounts, on the other hand, seem to Everyday People to be more transparent, easier to understand, and give easy access to their money.

Everyday People typically do not invest as a result of these beliefs. By not investing, instead putting their money in "safer" bank savings accounts, they believe they are being responsible by ensuring protection and security for their money. This in turn makes them feel good about their relationship with money. They may similarly prioritize paying down other expenses or debt with available cash flow in favor of using the same cash flow to invest.

Unfortunately, this is a misunderstanding of the advantages and relative safety and protection of investments.

In any given year, the stock market can be volatile, and it is true that the biggest difference between saving and investing is the amount of risk involved. The reason ROI is lower with saving is because little risk is involved. ROI is higher with investing because more risk is needed to produce higher returns. An investor is essentially rewarded for taking on that risk with better returns.

However, just looking at the average stock market return of 10% per year for nearly the last century, one can see that the risk of typical investing is relatively low. The key to investing is to take on *reasonable* risk. This involves proven investment behaviors such as long-term investing (as opposed to trying to time the market) and asset class diversification (as opposed to stock picking). These reasonable risk-taking behaviors provide the benefit of compound interest and the ability to weather periods of volatility. These are the investment behaviors of Truly Rich People.

##  YOUR NEXT MOVE

So how can Everyday People develop these habits? The way to get ahead is to start investing as early as humanly possible. The earlier you can begin, the better off you will be. The first step is learning more about investing. With so many different options and access to investing available, investing for beginners can be easy and straightforward. Once you understand the basics, the simplest way to start is to determine how much of your cash flow to invest and just do it. (If you do not have enough cash flow to invest, see the discussion in Chapter 5 about Everyday People who are truly just trying to make ends meet.)

Before I began investing, I had only a small rollover IRA from my previous company. I had not maxed out the available contributions to my 401k while I was there, nor was I making current contributions to this rollover IRA. Instead, I was using my cash flow to pay down my school loan debt. (I now know that I was using cash flow to pay down bad debt that I could have been using to invest with greater ROI.)

Once I knew better, I knew I needed to get into the market. Just as I had a system-based debt reduction plan in my budget, after I had reduced enough debt, I revised my budget to incorporate a new investment savings plan. This sounds way more sophisticated than it was. Through my earlier cash flow analysis, I had discovered that in addition to my overblown Rite Aid spending, I was spending way too much each morning at Starbucks. So I cut out the Starbucks runs and started making coffee at home to bring with me to work. I then put the $20 I was saving each week towards investing.

*Voilà!* That was my sophisticated investment savings plan. It truly was as simple as putting away $20 per week. It was not much, but over the course of a year, it came to over $1,000, and that was before compound interest.

But by that time, I knew how much opportunity towards building my wealth I was squandering by not investing, and did not want to wait to save a huge sum of money. I was fired up and wanted to get started investing right away. Many Everyday People believe there is a substantial minimum amount of cash needed to start investing. That simply is not true. You can begin investing with as little as $20.

In my case, I opened an online brokerage account which allowed me to invest a fixed dollar amount to purchase fractional shares rather than whole shares. A fractional share is less than a full share of an equity or Exchange Traded Fund (ETF). Fractional share investing allowed me to invest small amounts of money in expensive securities which were otherwise out of reach. I then set up recurring, automatic transfers of the $20 from my checking account to purchase the fractional shares each week. Like they said in the Ronco Rotisserie infomercial, all I had to do was "set it and forget it!"

Over time, as I continued to practice the habits (analyze my PFS, strategically budget, increase my cash flow and reduce my debt), I also began to max out my IRA contributions as an additional method of investing. Having gained an understanding of the power of cash flow, ROI, compound interest, and *good* versus *bad* debt, I realized that contributions to retirement accounts and certain other employee benefit investment options were as important and effective—if not more so—as after-tax investing, and I had not been taking full advantage of that.

When I ended my legal practice and went back to a corporate position as an employee, I immediately began to max out my 401K contributions and had an additional benefit of receiving employer-matched contributions. Next, when employee benefits selection time came around, I opted for a high-deductible health insurance plan. High-deductible health plans (HDHP) typically have a lower monthly pre-tax salary deduction for premiums than other health plans, but they have a much higher out-of-pocket minimum deduction for medical expenses, which is why many Everyday People do not select them.

However, if you are relatively healthy, and with careful analysis about your personal health and other circumstances, this can be a powerful additional investment opportunity. This is because the pre-tax income that would have otherwise been contributed to pay for the higher premium of an ordinary health plan is instead invested in a Health Savings Account (HSA). The money in the HSA is then available for use *if* a medical expense arises. However, the pre-tax funds in the HSA are put to work in the investment market.

**Health Savings Account (HSA):** A type of savings account that lets you set aside money on a pre-tax basis to pay for qualified medical expenses. By using untaxed dollars in a Health Savings Account (HSA) to pay for deductibles, copayments, coinsurance, and some other expenses, you may be able to lower your overall health care costs. HSA funds generally may not be used to pay premiums.

While you can use the funds in an HSA at any time to pay for qualified medical expenses, you may contribute to an HSA only if you have a High Deductible Health Plan (HDHP)— generally a health plan (including a Marketplace plan) that only covers preventive services before the deductible.

Some health insurance companies offer HSAs for their HDHPs. Check with your company. You can also open an HSA through some banks and other financial institutions. Healthcare.Gov Website

As compared to a regular health insurance plan, with the HDHP you gain two significant advantages: 1) more cash flow available for investing due to the lower premium, and 2) the additional cash flow for investing is pre-tax because it is directly deposited into the HSA. You end up taking the same amount of money you would spend prepaying for medical services not yet given, and possibly not even needed, to additional retirement investment savings with tax benefits and greater ROI. If you withdraw money from your HSA before you turn 65, and you're not using it to pay for qualified medical expenses, then you will have to pay income tax and a 20% penalty. But once you turn 65, that 20% penalty no longer applies. You can continue to use your HSA funds for medical expenses, avoiding taxes altogether on the withdrawals. But if you choose to withdraw the money for other purposes, you will just pay income tax. This is similar to how a traditional IRA works in terms of taxes. Just as with the intent of the IRA, by the time you use the HSA funds you will likely be in a much lower tax bracket.

I contribute the maximum amount allowable to invest in my HSA and have never had to use the investments for medical expenses, letting the investments grow tax-deferred. When medical expenses do arise, I still opt for using my other available after-tax cash flow if I can, rather than disrupt the long-term cycle and benefits of the investments and ROI in my HSA.

This habit of investing was the habit that unleashed the growth potential of all three previous habits. The ROI is irrefutable and has become the constant drive for me to invest. I routinely invest almost all additions to my cash flow from any source, such as increased compensation bonuses, tax refunds, and proceeds from the sale of any other investments. Investing is the key habit that made me Truly Rich.

## CHAPTER EIGHT

# HABIT 5

## Truly Rich People Seek Expert Advice

T ruly Rich People seek expert advice. On the other hand, most Everyday People try to manage their money all on their own.

As you now know from Chapter 4, Truly Rich People are honest about their financial picture. They are honest with themselves when they are not clear about financial planning and need a roadmap, or when they simply do not enjoy nor want to manage their finances.

They understand financial experts have the schooling, training, and, most of all, real-life experience working with diverse clients that they themselves do not. They know it takes time, talent, and effort to properly manage money and to make the best financial decisions. They know it is critical to ask the right financial questions, weigh the options, and implement a financial decision.

Most importantly, Truly Rich People understand financial planning is typically not their area of expertise. They know that even if they enjoy managing their financial plan, an objective and unbiased third-party perspective is beneficial. This is why Truly Rich People seek expert advice.

Many Everyday People on the other hand make very different assumptions about financial advisors. For instance, Everyday People often think wealthy people need financial advisors because they have a lot of money and large investment portfolios as compared to their simple assets. In addition, they assume advisor fees are hefty, and therefore only wealthy people can afford to pay them. They logically then assume they do not need expert advice.

The truth is you do not need to have large investments or significant assets to benefit from expert advice, and expert advice can be more affordable than you think. More on that in the pages to come, but let's first understand why it is important to have financial expert advice.

## REAL ANSWERS

Here are two great questions for Everyday People who do not seek expert advice:

- Who will guide and manage your financial future?
- What might you miss or overlook?

Here are the answers most Everyday People give:

- I'll handle it myself.
- I won't miss anything, or at least not anything too important.

For the first question, Everyday People who want to manage their finances must honestly ask themselves if they truly have the skills to do it alone. In the rare instance that they do, they should then ask themselves if they *want* to do this and if they really will *take the time* to do it. The answer to both of those questions is often no. That means that despite checking the box that they are managing their own finances, there is no true guidance and management for their financial future.

As for the second question, when Everyday People attempt to manage their financial future themselves, they often run into a problem: *they don't know what they don't know.* For instance, when Everyday People go it alone, they often face a common risk of not putting in place a solid and sustainable *growth strategy.*

Everyday People can greatly benefit from expert advice to help them become more organized, develop a financial plan with a sustainable growth strategy, and put that plan into action. Once a sustainable plan is in place, there are still financial decisions to be made and actions to take. An expert can assist in choosing the best actions and considering alternative paths. They can even illustrate options for you with risk simulations to help you visualize the consequences of certain financial decisions. Experts can help Everyday People comprehend how the actions in one area affect their overall financial plan.

Everyday People managing their own investments sometimes focus too much of their attention on taking action (such as getting in on an apparently amazing stock tip to get big financial rewards) and not enough attention on when *not* to act. For example, Everyday People could benefit from an expert advising them that while they are waiting for that amazing stock tip to appear, they just might be holding too much cash and missing out on the long-term gains that cash could provide if put to use in the market. The expert could make other important observations, such as an opportunity to consolidate investment accounts which could reduce costs, gain greater investment scale, and improve diversification. Most importantly, expert oversight can provide accountability for Everyday People and assist them in progressing toward their objectives as well as helping to revise plans when circumstances change.

Finally, as an insider in the financial industry, the biggest challenge I saw wealthy people grapple with in terms of their wealth was their own emotions. Emotional impacts range from preventing the creation of estate plans to wanting to prematurely sell investment holdings during market volatility. My most important responsibility as a financial advisor was to remain objective and help clients parse out their emotional-based actions from fact-based actions.

When Truly Rich People seek expert advice, they mitigate the consequences of potential risks and emotional impulses, maximize financial knowledge and time, and they gain peace of mind.

# ➜ YOUR NEXT MOVE

How can Everyday People develop the habit of seeking expert advice? The first step is to figure out what you need help with because there are many types of financial advice. You may need the advice of an accountant or a tax preparer to help with lowering income taxes, reviewing property taxes, and making sure all available tax deductions are taken. You might need an estate planning lawyer to ensure you are creating generational wealth for your family and your financial plan is not derailed at your death. You may need an insurance broker to protect you from unexpected events as you build your wealth. You may just want investment advice to get started investing or to help with your existing portfolio. You may need all of these experts.

If you do not know what you need, I suggest starting with a financial planner whose job is to help create a personalized plan to manage your budget and achieve your financial goals. A financial planner can then help you determine the additional expert advice you need and connect you to other appropriate experts.

The next step is to find the right person. Some Everyday People can be quite skeptical of financial advisors. They may think financial advisors are a "rip-off" or are going to steal their money. These Everyday People readily refer to situations like the Bernie Madoff scandal as confirmation of their fears. As with any important purchase or hire, you want to do your research, but the Madoff situation was and still is extremely rare. People with varying levels of wealth are advised by financial experts every day with great success in helping them with their financial planning.

The more common problem people have when selecting an advisor is engaging an advisor without enough experience or without specific experience in what you are looking to achieve. Not all advisers are alike. You want to find someone who is familiar with your level of wealth and also with the particular goals you have. For instance, if college planning is a major goal, you will want someone who has experience with that.

A good referral is worth a lot, so asking around can be a great way to find a good advisor. There are also digital apps that can match you with an advisor. There are even membership services that include unlimited access to professionals for investment management, retirement planning, college planning, debt management and reduction, insurance planning, and legacy and estate planning.

As for affordability, financial planners typically charge an annual retainer which tends to be $1,200 to $6,000 for a comprehensive financial plan. For investment management, the charge is typically a flat percentage of your total investment account balance which is usually between 0.25% to 1% per year. This fee is typically deducted from the investment assets in the account each year. Commission-based advisors receive commissions from the specific investments they sell.

However, you may be able to find a financial planner for less. Your credit card or financial institution may offer financial planning solutions to you as a free or discounted service for being a client. Many employers also offer financial planning solutions for free or at a discounted cost to their employees.

It is important to know that Truly Rich People are not blindly led by experts and their advice. Rather, they routinely seek expert advice and develop a close relationship with the advisors who provide it. While they allow the experts to do their job, they also ask important questions and make sure they fully comprehend the advice they are given. They also understand it is the expert's job to break things down as much as necessary for them to be engaged and informed, and they hold these experts to that accountability.

## FINANCIAL ADVISOR FEES

Many advisors charge based on how much money they manage for you, a fee structure called "assets under management," or AUM. Some advisors charge a flat fee — either per financial plan, per year or per hour — instead of a management fee.

| Fee type | Typical cost |
| --- | --- |
| Assets under management (AUM) | 0.25% to 0.50% annually for a robo-advisor; 1% for a traditional in-person financial advisor. |
| Flat annual fee (retainer) | $2,000 to $7,500 |
| Hourly fee | $200 to $400 |
| Per-plan fee | $1,000 to $3,000 |

The first time I sought expert advice was long before I became a financial advisor. I utilized the financial planning services offered through my credit card company. For a one-time fee of under $1,000, I had a dedicated person, Don, with whom I could discuss my financial goals. I shared my concerns about debt, and he helped me get a handle on my financial picture. It was Don who led me through a simple exercise that gave me an understanding of the importance of tracking expenses. As I revealed in Chapter 5, this understanding was critical to me beginning to live within my means (Habit #2).

The bottom line is this: seeking expert advice was one of the first steps that put me on the path towards becoming Truly Rich. And it may well be the first step for you.

## CHAPTER NINE

# HABIT 6

## Truly Rich People Envision Retirement

Truly Rich people envision their retirement. Everyday People fret and worry about retirement without a vision.

The successful clients I have worked with are the ones who envision what they want their lives to look like in the future. Some envision themselves traveling the world, while others plan to spend more time with family. All of them have a solid idea of where they want to live after retiring. Those who envision living somewhere other than their current home also envision how they will handle the move and what will happen with their current home. Some know they will sell their home to provide liquidity to purchase a different retirement home, so they begin the research for selling and purchasing these properties long before they retire. In short, they envision and prepare for no longer working.

Most Everyday People know they need to plan for retirement. How can they not? Everywhere they go they see television advertisements for financial institutions and their retirement planning services. They see real estate retirement complexes being developed in their neighborhoods. They may see their own aging parents and wonder if they will need to help them in retirement. They may hope they will not need the help of their children in their own retirement. Reminders of the importance of retirement planning are abundant. But most Everyday People are too overwhelmed to truly envision their retirement. They simply do not know what the end of their financial journey looks like. Worse, they often assume it will be bleak and they will not be able to stop working when they wish to. *Who would want to envision that?!* Instead, they blindly hope that somehow it will all work out.

Unfortunately, for far too many Everyday People, failing to plan and not having enough money for retirement will become the reality. The repercussions of Everyday People failing to save enough for retirement can manifest themselves in a variety of ways. Without investing for retirement, options become increasingly constrained for Everyday People, particularly if they do not own their home free of debt, resulting in limited options for where they can live after retirement.

As an example, elderly Everyday People without a retirement plan may need to take up a part-time job, give up their comfortable home for a small apartment, or move in with an adult child, placing significant financial strain on their children's lives and leading to relational resentment. Some may have to sell their house and move away from family to an area with a lower cost of living, while others may be required to spend down all of their assets to be eligible for Medicaid and live in an assisted living home.

While failure to plan for retirement may not result in such calamities all the time, it can still result in the death of the hopes of Everyday People. For instance, a lack of retirement planning and funds could mean Everyday People spend their retirement years working full-time or paying down debt instead of enjoying their time. It could also mean passing on their debt to family upon their death rather than creating generational wealth.

Another pitfall for Everyday People is assuming that they *can* work for as long as they may need to—and that *is* their retirement plan! The average retirement period is twenty-plus years. No one, Truly Rich People nor Everyday People, can predict the future and whether they will remain healthy enough to continue to work, or if work will even be available for them during that time. Planning to work forever is simply not realistic. It is the same as not having a plan at all.

Everyday People may assume that wealthy people envision their retirement because they will be able to afford their current lifestyle through their retirement without needing a plan. While it is true that some very wealthy people may have the funds to support their same lifestyle through retirement, as we saw with Brett in Chapter 2, even very wealthy people struggle with staying on track for retirement when they do not envision it. Truly Rich People with ample wealth have a financial plan which includes a specific plan to preserve that wealth so it is available for their retirement. Truly Rich People have both a clear vision for their future and a plan for accumulating the funds for it.

Envisioning the possibilities of a retirement lifestyle can actually be a step in the right direction for Everyday People who fear it. When they imagine what their retirement lifestyle will look like, it becomes easier for them to plan for the future. Simply spending time thinking about the ideal retirement can lead to better saving habits. In fact, studies have shown that those who envision their ideal retirement are significantly more likely to contribute at least 15% of their income to a retirement plan than those who do not.[1] Envisioning works, which is why it is a habit of Truly Rich People.

 **YOUR NEXT MOVE**

How can Everyday People develop this habit? There is much more to envisioning retirement than just thinking about vacations, time with family, and not working. We learned in previous chapters the importance of having an honest understanding of your financial picture, budgeting to live within your means, the increased ROI from investing versus simply saving, and the benefits that come from seeking expert advice.

What you discover through practicing those habits will influence how you envision your retirement, and how you envision your retirement will influence those habits. Let me say that again: What you discover through practicing those habits will influence how you envision your retirement, and *how you envision your retirement will influence those habits*. Having realistic goals when envisioning retirement is important. For instance, if you have lived paycheck to paycheck, with no savings or investments, but envision a retirement in which you will take multiple trips around the world every year, buy a big beach house for your family to visit, and hire a nursing staff to take care of you if your health declines, that is simply an unrealistic vision. A realistic set of possibilities for your retirement will allow you to more accurately determine what planning you need to do now.

Sometimes you may think you need significantly more retirement savings than you actually do, particularly if your current financial picture is strong and you envision retirement as simple as remaining in your home and taking a fishing trip every year. Envisioning can turn up unexpected results in this way, too. Either way, Truly Rich People envision retirement to bring them peace and financial ease, not to drastically reinvent their lives.

Envisioning a complete retirement in this way may seem intimidating, but it can be broken down into manageable pieces. Start by thinking about the different stages of retirement, such as the initial transition from full-time work to working part-time or consulting. Then envision what not working at all could be like and whether that will change where you want to live or how and with whom you will want to spend your time.

Finally, think about a potential stage of life where health, mobility, cognitive issues, or the loss of a spouse might influence your vision. Be sure to think about potential roadblocks in each stage and how you would address them, such as having to care for your parents or other people you may need to support or help during retirement. Helping children with down payments on a home and with wedding costs can be a desirable goal when planned for, but a retirement nightmare if not planned for. Once you have envisioned your retirement, you can then work backward to figure out what you need to do to get there.

The final step is to determine how well your current financial picture supports your vision. You can then create a separate retirement plan to bridge any gaps and ensure you stay on track. In addition to saving and investing separately for retirement, this plan should include consideration of estate planning, disability insurance, and business succession planning if you own a business. This is where seeking expert advice can be critical. Your savings, income, Social Security, investments, and insurance are all part of retirement planning. An expert can help you understand what is available and run simulations to stress test your vision.

## CREATIVE COMFORT

When I first envisioned my own retirement, I had one small rollover investment IRA account. I knew I had dropped the ball by not starting early with retirement planning. I simply thought I would just have to work until I turned ninety!

When I did the hard work of making a real plan, though, I knew instantly that my financial picture could not support my children's college tuition as well as my retirement vision. I assumed the best route was for my children to take school loans while I secured my retirement so that I would not be a burden on my children. It was a huge emotional hurdle for me to think about not paying for my children's college education the way my parents had paid for mine, and for my children to take on school debt knowing the burden my law school debt had given me.

But I talked this through with my financial planner (Habit #5!). Through his advice, I invested in a specific insurance vehicle for which the premium costs comfortably fit into my budget but would provide ample cash to supplement college tuition payments in the future. I then completed an estate plan and secured disability and life insurance to ensure that if anything happened to me, my children's college expenses and more would be covered. I gained invaluable comfort knowing that I was doing everything I could to give my children the best financial security I could without irresponsibly derailing my retirement plans.

Over the years I have adjusted my vision and plan for retirement as circumstances have changed. For instance, I know that while I envision retiring early, I will still work in some reduced capacity because it gives me joy. My advisor and I have adjusted for how this income-producing work in my retirement could positively impact my retirement plan. We regularly weigh other actions such as deferred compensation options and borrowing for consulting expenses and other business opportunities.

When I first thought about envisioning my retirement, it made me feel depressed and scared. But once I did the work, I was amazed at how it made me feel about my retirement. While in the beginning I could not envision everything I wanted, I came to envision true security and a sustainable plan. This then motivated me to do everything possible to broaden the possibilities of my retirement. I was empowered to make it happen. By consistently envisioning and adjusting my retirement plan, I have been able to get to a place where I now have a financial plan to ensure my desired vision of retirement. The comfort I feel about my current financial footing, and knowing I will maintain that footing in the future, is one of the reasons I am Truly Rich.

## CHAPTER TEN

# HABIT 7

## Truly Rich People Share and Receive
## Financial Information

Truly Rich People share and receive helpful financial information with other Truly Rich People. Everyday People
neither ask for nor share helpful financial information with
each other.

One of the most prevalent habits of Truly Rich People
is developing valued relationships for sharing and receiving
information that cannot be obtained anywhere else. Many
of the wealthy clients I have worked with create business
ventures and engage in investment opportunities that are
unparalleled to those available to the average person. A great
deal of their success and ultimate wealth comes from their
access to people who provide timely and valuable information which contributes to and accelerates the success of these
ventures and opportunities.

While wealthy people have many professional circles and wealthy peers, Truly Rich People purposefully establish a few extremely strong and strategic personal ties. They develop, cherish, protect, and leverage these ties. Truly Rich People understand that these close ties are their greatest currency. Truly Rich People work on these relationships every day to mutually provide exceptional insights and opportunities.

Unfortunately, most Everyday People do not ask for nor share helpful financial information with each other. As a result, they rarely have a true network of people with whom they can share and receive helpful financial information. They often do not know how to develop these authentic networks. Because money can be a loaded topic for Everyday People, many have been conditioned not to discuss personal finances. In addition, being transparent about money can feel vulnerable and open to judgment.

If Everyday People do discuss money, they sometimes inflate how good (or bad) their personal financial picture is, which is neither authentic nor helpful to anyone. Deceptions about finances allow us to avoid discomfort and maintain the status quo in a relationship.

There are many reasons Everyday People sometimes *inflate* their financial picture to others. For instance, it can be a defense mechanism in cases where Everyday People want to prove detractors wrong who minimize their accomplishments. It can be a distraction to make up for deficiencies in other areas of their life, or where they have shame or disappointment about their financial practices and want to prove their self-worth. It can be a coping mechanism to receive adoration they otherwise do not receive. It can even be a strategy, albeit a poor one, to climb up the financial status ladder by manifesting their desired wealth.

On the other hand, the reasons why Everyday People may *deflate* their financial picture can stem from cultural norms, feelings of embarrassment, wanting to fit in, gain sympathy, or even attempting to receive financial help from others.

It should come as no surprise by now that these are all aspects of an unhealthy relationship with money. While inflating or deflating their financial picture to others might not reflect nor directly impact how Everyday People manage their finances, the need to inflate or deflate is an indication that work still needs to be done on their relationship with money. It often is a result of feeling the need to demonstrate they are "keeping up with the Joneses." Furthermore, deceptions about their financial picture can be a significant impediment to building authentic close ties with others with whom they can share and receive helpful financial information.

## THE BENEFITS OF SHARING

Why is this so important? The financial benefits Truly Rich People give and receive in those relationships come in a variety of forms:

- Thoughtful and otherwise unavailable financial advice
- Referrals to experts
- Access to unique investment opportunities
- Connections for enhanced career opportunities

Most experts agree only about 30% of all new jobs are ever advertised, and typically, the more senior the position, the less likely the job is to be advertised. This means 70% of jobs are hidden roles that are filled through networking.

- Perspectives on industry trends
- Opportunity to compare wealth strategies
- A peek into personal tips and habits
- Access and connection to their network
- Unique business advice
- Referrals for business customers
- Viable potential investors for their business and investment ventures
- And much more!

While these benefits serve to enhance wealth, the benefits of sharing and receiving information in this way can also address problems and concerns such as getting out of a bad investment or business. For example, one of my clients had an extremely unique business for which there was no viable succession plan for the next generation. In addition, due to the way the business was structured and funded, she stood to lose money if she sold the business at that time, despite its success. She confided in and sought advice from a friend in her network. Because of their relationship and his familiarity with her and the strength of her business, he connected her to a friend in his personal network who was looking to enhance his similar business. They ended up with a merger of the two businesses but structured the deal in a way that allowed her to exit the day-to-day activity of her business and also retain her equity in the business until such time a buyout of her interest would result in a gain.

If these reasons are not enough to demonstrate the power of building a strong network, think about this: Studies have shown that your closest relationships can actually affect your level of wealth. In fact, these studies indicate that a person's income is typically similar or equal to the average income of the five people with whom they spend the most time! Now I am not saying that Everyday People should ditch their best friends and family and take up or fake new friendships with a bunch of rich folks to advance their wealth. Please do not do that. The simple point is, Everyday People should resist the need to demonstrate they are keeping up with the Joneses but must also be mindful of the company they keep.

Everyday People should ask themselves whether the habits they seek to develop for financial success align with the habits of those with whom they spend the most time. If not, it is important for them to strategically add people with such habits to their network. It is helpful to think of your entire network of relationships as your team with teammates having varying positions and skills. Just as your teammates can help you in various ways, you too can help them. As the saying goes, you all have to be in it to win it.

As you have now seen, Truly Rich People are honest about their financial picture, strategically budget to live within their means, leverage credit while managing debt, invest for the power of ROI and compound interest, seek expert advice, and envision retirement. Through these habits, they have gained invaluable insights and learned critical lessons. As such, they have a plethora of information that most Everyday People simply do not have.

When Truly Rich People develop close relationships with other Truly Rich People, they have the opportunity to tap into this information to apply to their own financial picture. Critically important, though, is that Truly Rich People understand they have gained their own invaluable insights and have learned their own critical lessons which are valuable to their friends. Truly Rich People understand this is an opportunity for them to receive *and* to share helpful financial information.

# ➲ YOUR NEXT MOVE

How can Everyday People develop this habit? It begins by strategically but authentically developing one or two close relationships with Truly Rich People. I call this networking for wealth.

There is a distinction between professional networking or mentoring and networking for wealth. All are important, but you should know the difference to maximize time and understand the different benefits. Professional networks, such as bar associations, are formal, open to most in the profession, and organized in line with the general objectives of the profession. Professional networks can be useful for education, peer contacts, and referrals within the profession.

Mentoring typically involves a one-on-one relationship with someone in your professional network with the goal of the mentor helping the mentee advance in their career. Networks for wealth are a few informal, very powerful, targeted, and cultivated deep relationships. The people in your network for wealth readily use their relationships to provide you with information and resources.

So many Everyday People have an inherent resistance to networking in general. Lack of confidence significantly contributes to such resistance. For some Everyday People, the thought of interacting with strangers can be paralyzing. Other

Everyday People may be shy, have a fear of rejection, or have an under-estimation of what they can contribute to others.

In addition to a lack of confidence, Everyday People often have a lack of understanding of how authentic networking happens. Everyday People may have misconceptions such as networking is boring, causes stress, takes too much time, does not work, and is a waste of time. They may also be misguided in expecting immediate results from their network and become frustrated and impatient if they do not see overnight results.

Other Everyday People may resist networking because they are frightened about being *sold to.* Truly Rich People have worked to break through their resistance and misconceptions.

The key to networking for wealth is to have the right motives when thinking about and developing a specific relationship. If you do this with the wrong intentions, such as getting a job, borrowing money, or just focusing on a person's level of wealth, you will fail. The purpose of the relationship should be to align and complement each other's experiences, skills, and resources. Two things that are key to note: 1) you must specifically ask for the help you need, and 2) you must proactively share information you have gained. The question to ask yourself is always, "How can I add value to this person?"

There are many effective and useful how-tos of networking that are beyond the scope of this book. A simple Google search or trip to your local bookstore or library can point you in the direction of fantastic articles on the best practices of networking for wealth.

Ideally, the person you seek to develop a relationship with is successful, someone you admire, and with whom you already have a connection or know in some capacity. For instance, it could be a colleague, your boss, a fellow board member on a board of directors, or an acquaintance through a social club, professional association, or community volunteering. While it is important to make a positive impact, it involves more listening and being genuinely interested in the other person and what you may be able to do for them. Then it becomes about authentically transforming that connection into a deeper relationship and establishing mutual trust.

This process takes time! Sometimes it takes years and that's ok. Truly Rich People do not network for wealth to get rich or to get rich quickly. They network for their mutual financial and emotional wealth.

A recent example of a benefit I received through networking for wealth was a referral to a personal coach. I have a close friend in my network, Jason, whom I have known for over a decade. We work in the same profession, and over the years have collaborated on projects, supported each other's businesses, and even became mutual clients of each other. In fact, he became my financial advisor. He recently began receiving lucrative media engagements, and his business jumped to a new level.

During one of our regular get-togethers, I asked him about how he got connected to the media engagements. He told me he began working with an extremely sought-after executive coach, Anthony Flynn, who gave him unique and customized advice about his business and then connected him to the right people for media opportunities. Jason then made an introduction to Anthony, whom I ended up engaging, as well. Through working with Anthony, I tapped into my desire to share what I have learned throughout my career, and—you may see where this is going—he pushed me to write this book!

By developing the strong habits previously discussed and building the right relationship with money, I knew I had valuable lessons and information to share with others, and that there were many more lessons and information from others that I could still benefit from receiving. I learned the value of taking the time to build fruitful relationships as the mechanism for this sharing and receiving. I see it as making deposits and building credits in a relationship bank account, and I recognize that the return is over the long term. That is what being Truly Rich is really about.

## CHAPTER ELEVEN

# HABIT 8

## Truly Rich People Purposefully Discuss Money with Family

T ruly Rich People make a habit of purposefully discussing money and wealth with their family. Everyday People rarely discuss money with anyone, especially their children.

Truly Rich People talk about money openly and frequently with their family. They know money has a significant impact on life, so they aim for financial transparency with their family to achieve an environment that promotes healthy communication around learning and understanding about money, especially their personal wealth.

Some Truly Rich People were themselves raised in such an environment or understand early on the importance of this environment when starting their own families. To achieve financial transparency and create a similar environment for their family, they discuss their financial picture with their partners before and throughout marriage. When their children are young, just as they communicate with them about kindness, nutrition, dangers, positive and healthy habits, and values, so too do they communicate with them about money. They do not do so in a blunt and jarring way, though; they do so in a natural way, making it a part of their ongoing discussions.

Good money values and information about their personal financial picture are interspersed throughout normal discussions. By doing so, money is not an awkward or taboo subject within their family. Over the years, Truly Rich People's family members gain an appropriate understanding of their family's income, debt, net worth, spending, saving, financial history, and the potential risks and hurdles to their financial picture.

In this way, the family members develop healthy values and expectations around money and their personal wealth. To ensure it continues as their children grow older, Truly Rich People have purposeful and consistent discussion and even family meetings to discuss matters of money and wealth.

As we saw with Habit #7, most Everyday People do not share and receive helpful financial information. Since they typically do not discuss money with anyone, it comes as no surprise that they do not discuss money with their family. For most Everyday People, no one taught or discussed money and personal finance with them. They just picked up what they suspected they needed to know along the way. So, the first time many Everyday People discuss money with family is when something terrible occurs, like the loss of a job, bankruptcy, or after a death.

## A FAMILIAR FAMILIAL PROBLEM

It is not only Everyday People who do not discuss money with their families, however. Many very wealthy people share the same behavior. Let's recall the characters Brett and May from Chapter 2. May developed her relationship with money without any purposeful discussion from her parents. While she observed and ultimately picked up her father's strong work ethic, without purposeful discussions with him, May was left in the dark about his intentions for their business as well as any money management values or lessons for the substantial proceeds of the sale of the business. This caused shock, disappointment, and feelings of inadequacy for May instead of the security Tony intended for her, creating a paralyzing relationship with money for May.

By contrast, the lack of purposeful discussions in Brett's family about the limitations on their wealth and expectations about their legacy was likely a significant cause for Brett's overspending and roller-coaster relationship with his personal wealth.

Why is it important to purposefully discuss money and wealth with family? We now know that Truly Rich People have a healthy relationship with money. Conversations with family about money or the lack of such conversations directly impact our relationship with money. Done in the right way, purposeful family discussions about money establish good communication, manage expectations, and demonstrate respect for all members of the family. In addition, if serious discussions about money become necessary, the family already has a strong foundation to weather it.

Purposefully not talking about money is a common pitfall of Everyday People, especially when it comes to their children. Some fear their children might share their financial information with friends, while others simply believe it is none of their children's business. Still others assume their children already know what they need to know.

Some Everyday People who have a strong financial picture do not want their children's motivation and work ethic to be stifled by the knowledge of a potential inheritance or by viewing their money as a safety net. And many do not discuss money because they are confused about money and finance and feel they are inadequately prepared to discuss it.

Of those who plan to discuss money with their children, most believe waiting until they are much older is best, and yet they still never do. Finally, when Everyday People do discuss money with their children, many are unable to appropriately teach them specific critical skills like investing, credit history, and retirement planning.

There is significant risk in waiting until children are older to start having these conversations or in believing their silence prevents their children from receiving information about their financial picture. This is because initial and even subconscious values about life are formed early on. Children learn values by observing the everyday actions of their parents and absorb both what parents say directly to them as well as what they hear parents say to others.

Children also pick up emotional cues from observing their parents' behaviors and tone. Children's values around money are therefore formed early on as well. They learn financial habits by observing their parents' financial habits.

Disengagement from topics of money merely leaves children to make guesses about money and their family's financial picture. This often creates confusion and can lead to feelings of uneasiness and insecurity around money. It can also give the impression that a family is wealthier or poorer than it actually is. Therefore, when Everyday People choose not to discuss money with children, they are still shaping their children's relationship with money.

Here is a simple example of this: Do you recall Nick and Penny from earlier? Nick's relationship with money is nothing like his parents' relationship with money. Nick's father grew up during the Great Depression witnessing and experiencing a great deal of financial suffering. As a result, when his father became financially secure, he made certain that he and his family took full advantage of the lifestyle it provided. His parents worked diligently and regularly on their financial plan, investing and building for the long-term while also enjoying the here and now.

As is often the case though, his parents rarely discussed money with Nick. If they did, they tended to emphasize how difficult it was to achieve their financial success and how easy it would be to lose it. Nick wants to feel secure and enjoy the money, but he is concerned that he will not be as good as his parents at safeguarding it. Worse, he fears he may become too comfortable and lose everything. In short, Nick's relationship with money is heavily influenced by his desire to avoid disappointing his parents.

And then we had Tamara, who built a healthy relationship with money and developed Truly Rich habits, quietly building her net worth to a level that would comfortably provide for her envisioned retirement and provide a substantial foundation for her children. Some Everyday People in Tamara's position, worried their children will not remain motivated to go to college and develop a career if they knew their net worth, do not talk about their personal financial picture with them. But Tamara understands her children may get this information anyway and therefore makes a point of talking about money with them.

Children as young as middle school age can get information on the value of their home, the cost of their cars and vacations, as well as their school tuition and household help's pay online. The accuracy or inaccuracy of this information can vary greatly, distorting the impression they develop. This same information is readily available to their friends, who may also share information with them. Children can obtain accurate information about their parents' wealth and still make inaccurate assumptions about their parents' intentions. By the time they are adults, they have formed their own opinion about their personal wealth and have already developed their relationship to their own personal wealth based on the lack of information shared with them.

If people discuss money with their children, they give them the best opportunity to never get on the financial roller coaster. When Truly Rich People purposefully discuss money with their family, they are focused on their family developing the best relationship with money.

 **YOUR NEXT MOVE**

How can Everyday People develop this habit?

> There are many effective and useful how-tos for discussing money with family and money education for families which are beyond the scope of this book. A simple Google search or trip to your local bookstore or library can point you in the direction of fantastic articles, apps, and online resources, including fun resources for children, such as interactive mobile apps and games. Many banks also have resources for children and educational-driven accounts.

The first step is to start early or start now. No matter your financial picture nor the age of your children, it is never too late to impart value and promote healthy communication, understanding, and learning about money for your family. You do not have to be a financial expert to have conversations about money with your children, siblings, and parents. You just need to have a plan. You can begin simply by sharing some of the insights you gained from reading this book. Then continue to share additional financial insights, methods, and experiences with your family on a regular basis.

If your children are very young, do not hand them financial books, give them too many details all at once, or tell them specific numbers about your personal financial picture. Make it fun and begin instead with simple concepts and values such as the difference between *needs* and *wants.* As they get older, move on to larger concepts, such as discussions about setting up a bank account, budgeting their allowance, the cost of college, how student loans work, credit, and credit history.

Along the way, start to reveal how much you get paid, how you spend your money, and your net worth. Share how you feel or felt about money and how money has benefited or harmed you. Encourage them to ask questions and resist keeping financial information from them. These are important moments when values about money can be taught.

If your children are adults (or you are the adult children in your family), discussing finances with adult children or parents could be critical. It is much better for these discussions to be had now, while everyone is mentally and physically healthy and to avoid difficult circumstances later. The more open discussions are, the less risk there is for conflict and disappointment.

As your family achieves financial transparency and you create an environment that promotes healthy communication, understanding, and learning about money, shift to more formal and consistent discussions, eventually getting to annual (or as often as you want or need) meetings. It is particularly helpful to make this shift prior to children going off to college and moving on to their own homes and families.

When the routine of having annual family meetings has already been established, it is much more likely such meetings will be respected, well-attended, and continued for the long term. With more formal meetings, it is important to have a clear understanding of what your family aims to accomplish in the meeting. The objective of consistent and purposeful meetings about money in this way is to limit shock, disappointment, and tensions about events and decisions that may impact your family's financial picture throughout the future.

As an example, Truly Rich People typically share their estate plans and business succession plans in family meetings well in advance of death and keep the family apprised of changes or external impacts to such plans. Truly Rich People make sure all family members (from the youngest to the oldest member) feel at ease with their family meetings and are comfortable asking questions to which they will respond frankly and honestly.

When my youngest daughter, Claire, was about four years old, I mentioned to her during a conversation at home that we could not afford something. She responded with "Then why don't you go to the ATM and get some more money?" So I began talking to my children about money when they were very young. I set them up with bank accounts, had discussions about savings, and gave them exercises for budgeting and charity. But I was not consistent with these activities throughout their childhood. More importantly, as we approached the pre-college years, it dawned on me that my discussions with my daughters were geared towards the specifics of money management, but I had not discussed our personal financial situation with them in any meaningful way. I had talked about the importance of their grades in relation to scholarships and the burden of school loans, etc. But it was apparent that although they had a clear understanding of my expectation of their going to college, they had no clarity on how college would be paid for, nor if and how it would affect my and their financial future.

By this time, I had already done the work on my own relationship with money, had been readily applying the 10 Critical Habits of Truly Rich People, and had accumulated wealth. But it was all locked up within me. I needed the importance of these discussions about college tuition to be more than an understanding of the process and mechanics of paying for college. It needed to be about all my children developing healthy values and expectations around money and their own personal wealth. So, I began to talk to them about our legacy with money.

I told them stories about the experiences of my parents and great-grandparents with money as well as my own stories. I took them through all our mistakes, hardships, and lessons we learned. Through many discussions, I started the process of imparting the knowledge, values, and skills upon which our family's wealth was built.

My purpose was—and still is—to give them a deep sense of responsibility so they can respect, protect, and preserve this legacy, and give them a sense of empowerment so they can enjoy and grow it for future generations. I want to give them the foundations they need to be Truly Rich.

## CHAPTER TWELVE

# HABIT 9

## Truly Rich People Are Philanthropic

Truly Rich People are philanthropic. Everyday People give money away.

Truly Rich People are generous and committed to many important causes, such as ending world hunger, addressing climate change, housing the homeless, fostering equality, supporting the arts, and generally helping people in need. They give in many ways. Simple examples include helping their neighbors and friends with errands, cooking meals, childcare, volunteering their time to an organization, donating their professional services (construction, land-scaping, financial management, or legal services), serving as a board member for nonprofit organizations, and giving cash donations to people and charities. Their giving provides critical aid to those in need and enriches their communities.

In addition to the beneficial aid for the recipients, giving also provides great benefits to Truly Rich People. Numerous studies have shown that helping others and giving money to charity increases a person's overall happiness and reduces their mortality rate. Giving to others directly and positively affects a person's satisfaction in life; studies also show that the more people give, the more satisfaction they feel.[1] Other benefits Truly Rich People receive by giving include the chance to meet new people, learn different skills, and model kindness, generosity, and social responsibility for others, especially their children.

As it turns out, Everyday People are just as generous and committed to important causes. The difference is in the ways Truly Rich People and Everyday People give.

Truly Rich People tend to be long-term and strategic regarding their giving. They often focus on making multiple gifts to help people over a number of years. They may not always see the immediate impact of their giving, but still receive the enriching benefits that charitable giving promotes.

An additional benefit Truly Rich People receive through their giving is income tax savings. We spend portions of our income on different things, including housing expenses, food, entertainment, etc. It is the same when we spend a portion of our income to make a charitable donation. However, income that is used for such charitable purposes is viewed and treated differently under the US Internal Revenue Code than income used for those other expenditures.

While income is generally taxable, a charitable tax deduction may be taken so that a person does not have to pay income tax on the portion of their income they have used for charitable purposes. These income tax deductions can significantly reduce the income tax otherwise owed, essentially increasing cash flow.

Truly Rich People also engage in *planned giving*, a term describing the strategic use of specific transactions and vehicles (such as a trust) for charitable purposes. Planned giving provides flexibility and control to donors. For example, certain transactions allow a donor to donate different kinds of assets other than cash, such as a car, artwork, a boat, or even real estate. This not only provides flexibility but also preserves cash flow.

Another benefit of planned giving is the ability to receive tax benefits on other types of taxation (i.e. estate tax, gift tax, and capital gains for income tax purposes) in addition to the charitable income tax deduction benefit for income taxation.

There are numerous planned giving vehicles which can basically be grouped into three categories. Outright Gifts which are easy, direct, and require one transaction, Life Income Gifts which provide investment opportunities for the donor, and Asset Protection Gifts which are more geared towards tax protection and generational estate planning. Just like a cash gift, these planned giving vehicles provide an income tax charitable deduction equal to the value of the gift. However, most of the vehicles do not affect cash flow at all.

Tax strategies for giving can have many complexities. When done right, it can have significant benefits, and when done wrong, it can have significant and often costly risks. This book is not intended to provide tax planning advice and strategies.

Truly Rich People see charitable giving as an integral part of their budget and overall financial plan. They strategically plan for and incorporate charitable income tax deductions. In addition to taking advantage of these deductions and other benefits of planned giving, Truly Rich People are disciplined in their giving frequency and consistency, tracking their donations, setting limits on amounts, and doing due diligence. Giving in all these ways is described as *philanthropy*.

Truly Rich People have the habit of philanthropy, promoting both the emotional and the financial benefits of giving. They are diligent in ensuring that their good intentions of giving do not derail their other Truly Rich Habits. This balance is a sign of the healthy relationship Truly Rich People have with money.

## WHY PHILANTHROPY?

Everyday People tend to take a more upfront and short-term approach to helping organizations and people in need. They are charitable, but they also tend to be less disciplined in their giving in terms of consistency and tracking or setting limits; they give spontaneously rather than as an integral part of their budget and overall financial plan.

Some Everyday People give in this manner because they want their giving to be driven by compelling emotions, while others take great joy in being able to provide immediate relief to people and see their impact right away. Finally, Everyday People tend to view giving more broadly as simply helping other people, rather than as a strategic charitable giving plan. For instance, in addition to charitable organizations, Everyday People often give money to family, friends, and other individual people, spontaneously giving money away.

If all types of giving are good, why is Philanthropy important? We often think about how our negative or selfish behaviors, such as overspending, can impact our ability to achieve financial success and stability. Most of the Truly Rich Habits discussed in this book are geared toward addressing such behaviors. It is harder though to think about how our good intentions and positive behaviors can have a similar impact. When Everyday People set off with the goal to do good through their giving, they almost always see it as a separate focus from their financial goals. However, the foundation of both goals is money. Therefore, both giving and financial success are intrinsically linked, whether we think that way or not.

What is especially illuminating is that when Everyday People give without having a giving budget, they often give more than they can afford or intended. In the absence of structure, many Everyday People simply end up being too generous and succumbing to the pressures of in-the-moment requests, particularly from compelling or important people in their lives. When Everyday People give in this manner, they run the risk of impeding both their financial and giving goals. Philanthropic giving provides strategic planning. The lack of that strategic planning can delay and even prevent Everyday People from achieving their financial goals.

# ➲ YOUR NEXT MOVE

How can Everyday People develop the habit of philanthropy? The good news is that it does not require Everyday People to change their desire to give. They just need to think more strategically about *how* they give. It begins by applying many of the Truly Rich Habits already discussed.

Start with Habit #1 by being honest about how much and to whom you want to give. Apply Habit #2 of living within your means by understanding what your previous giving looked like as a part of your cash flow analysis. You will then want to determine how much you are able to give, knowing that the amount must fit within your overall spending and cannot exceed the budget you created for your total cash flow.

If your budget does not allow you to give as much as you want, perhaps look to incorporate strategies similar to the debt reduction plan or investment savings plan found with Habit #3. Look to Habit # 4 to possibly increase your charitable ROI through planned giving investment vehicles. Think about how to increase ROI for the charity too, through such vehicles and with gifting investment assets. Do not forget to think about Habit #6 and how your retirement vision incorporates your charitable goals.

If you envision yourself devoting substantial time in retirement to volunteering, you might delay some giving now to increase your net worth goals. Finally, applying Habit #5, consult with an expert to advise you on the planned giving opportunities and tax benefits that may be available to you.

A final note on tax benefits: Try not to get hung up on political arguments. These arguments say charitable tax deductions are great for the wealthy but not for the poor. This is because a person must have sufficient income against which to claim the charitable deduction. Thus, the argument made is that people who earn a lot of money are the only ones who can truly take advantage of the charitable tax deduction. However, unless Everyday People are planning to make huge charitable gifts, they most likely have enough income to be strategic about giving and therefore can also claim the deduction. The inequity with who is able to claim the deduction is more apparent at the very upper and lower ends of the wealth gap.

Another argument suggests that people who get tax benefits from giving only do it for the tax benefits, passing judgment on motive and purpose of these types of givers. And some people view people who strategically use tax benefits as bad actors who are doing something wrong or even illegal.

Truly Rich People think about and address these arguments and types of thinking in many ways:

- Many Truly Rich People agree that the tax system does seem to have a lot of loopholes and inequities that are worth addressing. Those who feel this is an important endeavor are active about it and take advantage of opportunities to be involved in transformative initiatives that could bring about change.

- Truly Rich People can walk and chew gum at the same time, though. The tax benefits provided under the Internal Revenue Code are legal and available to everyone who qualifies. Therefore, Truly Rich People leverage solid laws which are beneficial to them while also taking steps to improve the access and applicability for everyone.

- Truly Rich People keep their eyes on the prize. The use of tax benefits and other strategic ways of giving through philanthropy is still giving! Truly Rich People focus on their purpose and know that their giving makes a difference to people in need and to important causes.

- Truly Rich People know that philanthropy ensures the longevity of their ability to give.

> Although they sound similar, "tax avoidance" and "tax evasion" are radically different. Tax avoidance is legal and involves structuring your transactions to receive tax benefits that lower your taxes. Tax evasion is a crime that involves deceit, subterfuge, or concealment to attempt to lower your tax.

When I shifted from being just charitable to being philanthropic, I began with small, purposeful changes. I incorporated a philanthropy spending amount in my overall budget. I determined in advance where my philanthropic spending would go for the year and worked with my accountant to utilize tax benefit-driven planning strategies.

To allow for some unplanned giving here and there, I also included a small additional amount to my overall budget for small donations. But I made rules about this unplanned donation spending portion, such as never giving cash (for expense accountability) and never giving to people going door-to-door.

Most importantly, if a purpose or cause was compelling, urgent, or moved me in some other way to give, I stuck to being philanthropic by adjusting my budget through other expense reductions to make room for it. I did not overspend.

Truly Rich People know charitable giving and philanthropic giving are equally important parts of the larger process and purpose of helping people. Philanthropic giving can meaningfully enhance charitable giving, such as when a nonprofit organization mainly funded through planned giving efforts makes grants to small independent charities. Similarly, charitable giving can meaningfully enhance philanthropic giving, such as giving a ride or transportation money to someone who could not otherwise get to a philanthropically funded center.

Therefore, Truly Rich People remain flexible and seize both charitable and philanthropic opportunities. I can think of no better way of being Truly Rich than promoting both the emotional and the financial benefits of giving through philanthropy.

## CHAPTER THIRTEEN

# HABIT 10

## Truly Rich People Help Others with Their Financial Futures Only After Securing Their Own

T ruly Rich People help others with their financial futures only after securing their own. Everyday People often help others to their own financial detriment.

I have worked with many wealthy clients who use their financial success to help others build financial wealth. Earlier, we saw the many ways Truly Rich People help others financially by simply sharing information.

Some of my clients were professional money managers and investors themselves who assisted their clients with growing their assets and managing their wealth via their profession. Other clients shared valuable information with friends about investing or personal business ventures they might be considering. Some clients even went beyond sharing information and actually helped people by making financial gifts, lending money, or creating trusts for their benefit. Still other clients helped people by funding their business ventures. At a minimum, most of my clients helped their children by assisting them in building wealth as well as by teaching them how to handle the wealth they would ultimately need to manage.

Many Everyday People also use their financial success to help others build financial wealth in these same ways if they are able to do so. But many more Everyday People have the best of intentions yet have not fully secured their own financial futures. Therefore, they are not truly in a position to help others.

Notwithstanding this lack of financial security, some of these Everyday People may have more money—or are perceived to have more money—than other Everyday People in their community. As a result, these Everyday People offer financial help to others because they believe they *should*, even if doing so is to their own financial detriment. Let's call these Everyday People "Everyday Benevolents." Everyday People tend to have a greater expectation of Everyday Benevolents to *share the wealth*. Likewise, Everyday Benevolents often have a greater expectation of themselves to share the wealth with their friends, family, and communities.

Consequently, often in group settings, Everyday Benevolents feel they *need to* or are *expected to* contribute financially in greater ways than anyone else, whether to individuals in the group or to the group as a whole.

For instance, Everyday Benevolents often pick up the tab for everyone, invite others on vacations and pay all the expenses, loan others money, cover others' debts, contribute to or invest in their friends' or family's business and investment ideas, and generally try to elevate the group's financial status.

While this greater expectation can sometimes be fueled by the pressure of selfish greed or jealousy of other Everyday People, it is typically fueled more often by common misunderstanding. I discussed earlier in Chapter 5 regarding Habit #2 how Everyday People may see others living a life of luxury and think that if they, too, simply had a lot of money, they would not have to worry about anything else and could spend freely. They believe they would certainly share the wealth if they had what they believe others have.

However, in that chapter, I cautioned to not let the way other people live and spend their money fool you. No one can truly know the actual financial picture of others and what others can afford to spend. Everyday People typically can only see what tangible things Everyday Benevolents have or spend. They also do not know if and how Everyday Benevolents are already providing financial help to others. Therefore, Everyday People often make assumptions about what they *believe* an Everyday Benevolent in their group can effortlessly afford to contribute based on this limited information. However, even if one appears to live a life of luxury, they may not be able to simply share the wealth all the time with all their friends and family when such sharing is outside their budget. It is simply another type of overspending.

The desire to share the wealth can be compelling though, especially if there is a belief that by sharing, Everyday People are helping their friends and family to secure their financial futures. Therefore, whether it is out of genuine desire, pressure, guilt, or just not knowing how to say no, it is understandable that overspending on friends and family by Everyday People in this way is common. This type of benevolent thinking is understandable and perhaps even admirable in a sense, but it tends not to be based on actual financial ability.

Very wealthy people can also have this benevolent thinking or feel the same pressure. I also briefly discussed in Chapter 5 how wealthy people can end up not being able to sustain their wealth, as often happens with lottery winners. In fact, one of the main causes for lottery winners losing their winnings in a short period of time is that they feel obligated to share it with friends and family in an unsustainable way, swiftly depleting their financial future.

But it can be the same problem for more traditional wealthy people, too. Nearly all wealthy clients I worked with are approached by friends and family to seek out a grant or investment of some kind. Sometimes the request comes from a charity, but mostly not. Either way, the cause is always compelling because it appears that only with the clients' money will the charity or individual be able to secure a sound financial future.

Some clients would bring these requests to me to consider as a part of our overall wealth management and investment discussion. As their advisor, I would often have to explain that the request was not in their budget, fell far outside of their investment risk tolerance, or did not have a strong ROI. Unfortunately, due to the compelling nature of the request, all too often the client had already made a commitment or promise to contribute prior to our discussion. Then came the difficult task of the client having to back out of the commitment or live with the consequences.

This is why Truly Rich People help others with their financial future only after securing their own.

What does that really mean though? The Truly Rich People I worked with were prepared for these types of requests. They typically had a combination of a predetermined budget allocation for such requests, a consistent process for making the decision to help, and a well-rehearsed discipline in handling such requests. As an example, when it came to friends and family asking for a loan, investment, or even a gift, my Truly Rich clients' standard response was that all business and investment discussions were handled in a formal manner and together with their advisor. In other words, no decisions to give money would be made on the golf course or at a child's birthday party. That way their advisor could have an objective and direct conversation along with the client *and* the requesting friend or family member to analyze the request and, more importantly, be able to say *no* when appropriate.

The importance of this discipline is not simply to be mean, to always say *no*, or to not share the wealth. In fact, there are many instances where such requests of Truly Rich People are appropriate, and Truly Rich People readily fulfill them. However, requests that have the potential effect of derailing the financial objectives of Truly Rich People are simply not fulfilled, because Truly Rich People understand that in order to help others, they have to first be in a position themselves to help.

You might think this sounds selfish or uncaring. However, think about the type of leader you would want to follow during a difficult time. You would likely want a person you could trust and respect based on how they handled themselves in their own difficult times. You would want someone who could provide guidance and support based on their deep experience with the situation. If they could not meet their own needs in such difficult times, it would be questionable whether they are the right person to lead you through such times.

A financial leader can only provide quality guidance and support to others by making sure they are financially able to do so. For instance, next-generation education (a type of customized training for descendants of wealthy people to learn how to manage, maintain and build wealth) is one of the important services I provided to my clients as an advisor. Taking this extra step to prepare children for the responsibilities of financial wealth and success is a critical form of helping others. If you recall, in Chapter 10 regarding Habit #7 I discussed the common resistance people of all sorts have to doing this.

But my Truly Rich clients understood and embraced the reality that in our work together we first needed to focus on and secure the management of *their* wealth before embarking on next-generation education for their children. They understood that we needed to first ensure they cultivated best practices and behaviors, including honestly understanding their financial picture, in order to pass those same healthy behaviors on to their children. They understood that if we started with the education of their children prior to their full embracing and understanding of the things they needed to do to preserve and maintain their wealth, that the education for their children would neither be complete nor as successful as it could be. In other words, Truly Rich People help others with their financial future only after securing their own.

This is a particularly difficult behavior for Everyday People to develop and stick to, though, especially when it comes to their immediate family. As an example, this is why so many Everyday People fail to save for their future and even use their retirement funds to pay for their children's college education. When doing so, Everyday People essentially put their own financial future at risk to pay for their children's current expenses.

What is wrong with postponing our own financial achievement to assist our children with their present expenses and relieve their future financial burdens? Perhaps nothing, if you truly are assisting your children by doing this. However, the reality is that when Everyday People reach retirement age with no retirement funds to fall back on, they may actually end up increasing the financial pressures on their children if their children must now share the burden of supporting them during their retirement years. This can be a major hindrance with a significant impact on the potential wealth and long-term financial objectives of their children.

In the end, the unfortunate consequence of Everyday People failing to secure their own financial future before helping their children is they have not actually helped their children at all. Cutting into your smaller, unfinished financial plan means less for you and less for those you want to help.

An analogy to the common air travel procedures during flight which most of us are familiar with is the simplest way to think about this. For every flight, there is a crew whose sole mission is to get the plane (and you) safely from point A to point B. The crew is fully prepared and trained on how to handle unplanned disturbances and dangers between the two points, ranging from minor maintenance issues to bad weather, from unruly passengers to crash landings that could impede the mission. The crew is trained to understand that these disturbances and dangers may be unavoidable, and therefore, the only way to successfully complete their mission is to have strict and consistent procedures in place.

One such procedure is in regard to oxygen masks. If you have ever flown on a commercial plane, you have likely heard the flight attendant describing the procedure to follow if the pressure in the cabin should change and the use of oxygen masks becomes necessary:

> Reach up and pull the oxygen mask towards you. Place the mask over your nose and mouth and secure it with the adjustable elastic band to ensure a snug fit. If traveling with others who need assistance, it is important to *secure your own mask first before assisting others.*

If you do not secure your own oxygen mask first, your effectiveness in helping other people is severely compromised and failure is inevitable. A person not wearing an oxygen mask is in greater danger of losing oxygen and passing out than if they are wearing an oxygen mask. If a person passes out while trying to help someone else put on an oxygen mask, both people will be in a compromised state with the possibility of neither of them getting enough oxygen to survive.

The flight attendant does not look up or learn this procedure just prior to an emergency deployment of oxygen masks, nor does the flight attendant wait until an emergency is at hand to inform everyone of this procedure. Rather, the flight attendant informs everyone of this procedure prior to take-off of every flight, well ahead of any potential need to deploy oxygen masks. Whether the need to deploy the masks arises or not during the flight, this procedure is critical because of the compelling desire we all have *not* to secure our own oxygen masks before helping others. It simply is not our first instinct. Rather, our initial response is to protect others, especially the ones we love, by doing anything to make sure they are safe before even thinking about turning back to help ourselves.

It is a similar response when it comes to finances, and Truly Rich People understand how difficult it can be to resist the instinct. Therefore, Truly Rich People take consistent and necessary steps to ensure that they are in a position to help others before doing so. When Truly Rich People help others with their financial future only after securing their own, they serve as *leaders* by demonstrating strong financial behavior, and as *teachers* by showing others how to achieve similar financial success. They ultimately provide *more* help to others who need it.

# ➡ YOUR NEXT MOVE

So how can Everyday People develop this habit? The primary stage of developing the habit is securing your financial future, which requires four important steps:

1. Know your final destination.

2. Understand and follow the route you will take to get there.

3. Put strict and consistent procedures in place to get you to your destination even in the event of unplanned circumstances.

4. Achieve your specific financial goals, thereby becoming Truly Rich.

The good news is that on your journey to Habit #10 you have already learned how to accomplish the first three steps from earlier chapters.

The route you will follow to become Truly Rich is the path of building the right relationship with money. The strict and consistent procedures you will put in place to safely get you there are The Ten Critical Habits of the Truly Rich. Once you have your financial destination and route mapped out with all the procedures in place, the fourth step is to make sure you get there!

This is what securing your oxygen mask is all about. It is not enough to simply know your destination, the route, and the procedures if there is still potential for you to change course, not follow the route, or stray from the procedures in the event of external pressure. You must stick to the plan.

Only after you have secured your financial future are you in a position to proceed to the second stage of Habit #10—being able to help others with their financial future. However, it is critical in this stage that you objectively evaluate each request or opportunity to help others, including your own desire to share the wealth, and do not become an Everyday Benevolent, which could jeopardize the financial future you have secured. Truly Rich People do this by establishing a set of objective guidelines ahead of time. This can be as simple as abiding by a no-exception monetary limit already incorporated into your budget, by consistently designating and engaging an objective third party to help you analyze each opportunity, or by following a prescribed process to get to a *yes* or *no* decision.

Finally, do not overlook that as a Truly Rich Person, the help you provide to others is not, nor should it be, confined to monetary action only. In fact, financial help given to others in monetary form by Truly Rich People may never be perceived by some recipients as enough. You may be familiar with the quote, "Give a man a fish and feed him for a day. Teach a man to fish and feed him for a lifetime." That means it is more beneficial to equip and empower others to become self-sufficient than to keep them reliant on your ongoing donations. Truly Rich People provide financial help to others in many forms other than monetary help, including the previously discussed Truly Rich Habits of sharing financial information, purposefully discussing money with family, and being philanthropic.

Truly Rich People know that these forms of help are often significantly more valuable to the people they help, which is a sign of being Truly Rich.

## CHAPTER FOURTEEN

# TRUE PROGRESS

At this point, I hope you feel motivated to begin cultivating the Ten Critical Habits of Truly Rich People. To create meaningful change, you need to be both energized and driven. If you have been putting off dealing with your financial habits in the past, now is the time to act.

It is also critical to understand that, while motivation is needed, simply desiring to improve your financial situation will not suffice. Becoming Truly Rich entails putting in the effort required not only to achieve financial wealth but also to achieve emotional wealth. By now you have seen that money can trigger a range of emotions. We make decisions about money that impact our financial situation, and these impacts, in turn, affect our feelings and future behaviors.

No one is entirely rational when it comes to money. However, our relationship with money is strongly tied to the financial habits we unknowingly establish around our financial management. Therefore, it is no surprise that unhealthy relationships with money lead to unhealthy financial habits, and healthy relationships with money lead to healthy financial habits.

It is also no surprise that although we want to improve our financial picture, we often do not make sustainable changes. We may pick up a good financial habit and start to practice it here and there, but something always manages to distract us. The habit gets quickly forgotten.

New habits may be good, but they do not necessarily change the old habits. We may spend a lot of time looking for new solutions but very little time working on our current relationship with money. We do this because most of us do not know what is required to develop that healthy relationship. This is the hard, but rewarding, work of building emotional wealth.

To build emotional wealth, it is necessary to become aware of our emotions (and those of our family) that are tied to money, because without awareness, those emotions will tend to override rational thinking and drive our actions. But it is also necessary to keep in mind that these emotions are not necessarily bad; they simply reveal what we are afraid of, what we are passionate about, and what genuinely matters to us.

The key is to become aware of our emotions and then harness them to tackle what we need to face. We are challenged not only to *unlearn* what has not worked in the past but also to put ourselves in settings that will reaffirm the new connection we are trying to replace.

We cannot achieve emotional wealth until we evaluate and modify our relationship with money. Without emotional wealth, we cannot begin to put into action new habits learned to develop financial wealth. Becoming Truly Rich requires both; it is a cyclical process.

When Everyday People address their relationship with money and achieve emotional wealth, they are poised to develop the essential habits to achieve financial wealth. I say *poised* because even with emotional wealth, forming new habits takes time and discipline. Studies show that it takes more than two months on average before a new behavior becomes automatic, but this varies greatly depending on the individual, the behavior, and the circumstances. It is critical to be aware of the work required to cultivate the Ten Critical Habits of Truly Rich People. Becoming Truly Rich is a marathon, not a sprint, and it is ok to take your time to truly develop one habit at a time.

Think back to some of the stories I shared in this book. Imagine if those people had done this necessary work to change their relationship with money and build emotional wealth. Imagine what might have happened if they implemented the Ten Critical Habits of Truly Rich People.

For instance, recall Brett, the sixty-year-old millionaire who appeared to the outside world as if he were living a life of fame and fortune, but in reality, was on the brink of losing most of his wealth. Imagine if Brett focused on his emotional wealth as much as he focused on his financial wealth. Imagine if he had examined the emotional habits he gained from his relationship with money as well as the emotional habits he gained from his parent's relationship with money.

Brett was expected to uphold the reputation of his family name and legacy, but his inherited wealth—through no doing of his own—was significantly lower than his father's wealth which had fueled the lifestyle Brett grew up in. Brett did not feel he nor his children were doing enough to uphold the legacy, and as a result, he overspent and used his financial wealth in an attempt to feel greater self-worth.

Imagine if Bret understood how not working on his relationship with money was keeping him on a financial rollercoaster. Imagine if through this examination he had gained a deep understanding of what was emotionally important to him versus what was financially important to him and could detangle the two. Imagine if he used this emotional wealth to develop habits to be honest about his financial picture to see that his trust income was not enough to support his lifestyle, allowing him to live within his means and see that he did not need more money.

If you recall, Brett's adult children were not well-positioned to generate their own wealth. Brett started three new businesses with them in the hopes of generating financial success for them. Imagine what Brett's children would have gained if Brett had purposefully discussed money with them and had demonstrated emotional wealth. The businesses in the end did not generate the wealth Brett was expecting. Instead, they were losing money, ultimately becoming a burden on Brett's personal finances. Imagine if Brett had helped his children with their financial future only after securing his own.

It is true that Brett already had extraordinary financial wealth. One might ask why I included his story if I wrote this book for Everyday People. I did so because Brett's story is a vivid example of the importance of building emotional wealth before you can become Truly Rich, even if you already have financial wealth. But you do not have to look far to see an example of what happens when Everyday People achieve emotional wealth.

Before I achieved emotional wealth, I was an Everyday Person subconsciously believing money and wealth had a direct impact on creating emotional experiences of belonging and connection to family and life. Once I had detangled what makes me emotionally rich from what makes me financially rich, I was able to focus separately on the habits I needed to establish to steadily accumulate, maintain, and enjoy financial freedom. As a result, I became a millionaire without even noticing it. But as stated at the start of this book, I do not define myself as a millionaire, and neither should you. That is an irrelevant status, an artificial goal, and a meaningless term. What I am is *Truly Rich*.

My intention in sharing these lessons is not to make you a millionaire, although I do believe financial wealth is frequently an unintended consequence. My true intention is for these lessons to help you to become empowered in your life by changing your relationship with money and to begin using your finances as a tool to achieve success in all aspects of your life, rather than considering the level of your wealth as an achievement in and of itself.

My hope is that you will find that by doing so, your happiness and sense of purpose will not be intrinsically linked to your financial success. My hope is for you to become Truly Rich.

# THE IMPACT OF GENDER AND RACE ON WEALTH

I want all Everyday People to be able to profit from the lessons presented in this book. As a black woman, though, it is crucial for me that this book be particularly accessible and useful to women, especially black women.

As you will discover, I have learned much from clients, coworkers, friends, and family members. But I have also made a lot of missteps, encountered many hurdles, and missed some opportunities on my own road to becoming Truly Rich. Many of these mistakes and hurdles are common ones that any of us might come across on a daily basis. But others, I have come to understand later in life, were directly related to being a black woman. It is my hope that women and women of color, in particular, will benefit from and learn from my failures and successes in dealing with these hurdles. I know how beneficial and life-changing it would have been for me as a young adult to have had the insights and information I have gained over the last few decades and captured in this book.

While this message is essential to me on this personal level, it is also critical for our society as a whole if we are truly committed to achieving diversity, equity, and inclusion for *all* Everyday People.

From a historical perspective, wealth can be generational. But without the same opportunity to accumulate wealth due to issues like gender and race bias and discrimination, the ability to build wealth and pass it down to your family is significantly impacted.

Now I am not naïve enough to think that a few lessons from me in the previous chapters can magically change these very real obstacles. I do believe, though, that sharing my journey and the wisdom I have acquired may help people change behaviors in *themselves,* which in turn may help them increase the odds of building financial richness.

Ten Critical Habits of Truly Rich People you learned in this book covered topics such as the importance of honestly knowing your financial picture, getting comfortable with investing, realistic retirement planning, discussing money with others, and avoiding negative charitable giving tendencies.

These habits are often challenging for Everyday People to develop. When you layer in additional gender and race-based barriers, it can be significantly more challenging for people of color, women, and especially black women to develop these same habits. In addition to these barriers, gender and race-based cultural practices can also cause us to develop behaviors that are contrary to the Ten Critical Habits of Truly Rich People.

## WOMEN AND WEALTH

In general, women have been coming into their own with regard to wealth in the US. In 2009, *Harvard Business Review* concluded, "Women now drive the world economy."[1] This was based on a survey that revealed women at that time controlled $20 trillion globally in annual consumer spending and predicted that figure would climb as high as $28 trillion over the following five years. The article also revealed that total yearly earnings for women at the time were $13 trillion and could reach $18 trillion over the same period.

A few short years later, a 2015 *Business Insider* article declared that women had overtaken men and controlled more than half of all U.S. wealth based on a study that revealed women controlled 51% of personal wealth in the U.S..[2] A study published in 2020 confirmed this predicted trend for women and concluded that over the next five years there will be a significant shift in financial and economic power toward women.[3]

The positive trend is similar with regard to women in business. According to a recent study by the Bureau of Labor Statistics, women make up 47% of the workforce and women-owned companies represent over 40% of registered businesses worldwide.[4] In addition, compared to the 300 new male-owned businesses launched daily, 1,821 new female-owned businesses are launched daily according to the annual State of Women-Owned Businesses report commissioned by American Express.[5]

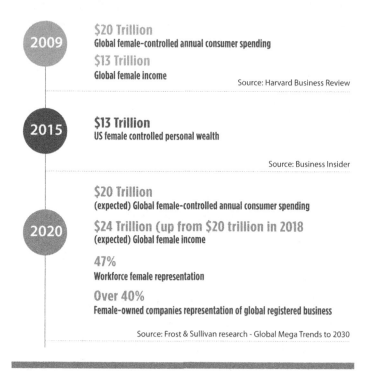

## FEMALE FINANCIAL STATISTICS

**2009**

**$20 Trillion**
Global female-controlled annual consumer spending

**$13 Trillion**
Global female income

Source: Harvard Business Review

**2015**

**$13 Trillion**
US female controlled personal wealth

Source: Business Insider

**2020**

**$20 Trillion**
(expected) Global female-controlled annual consumer spending

**$24 Trillion (up from $20 trillion in 2018**
(expected) Global female income

**47%**
Workforce female representation

**Over 40%**
Female-owned companies representation of global registered business

Source: Frost & Sullivan research - Global Mega Trends to 2030

Yet despite these tremendous trends, in my experience advising women clients over the years, many women struggle to achieve financial and emotional wealth. During my career, I became certified as a women's business advocate. Through this certification training, as well as the experiences of my women clients, I came to understand some of the gender-based cultural differences and hurdles women have.

For instance, many married women defer to their spouse when it comes to handling the household finances. Some do this because they believe they are not capable of handling finances, while others may do it simply for ease or because their spouse has always handled the finances. Whatever the reason, it leaves women ill-equipped to understand their finances or develop behaviors that could help them become Truly Rich.

This can be especially difficult if these women are widowed and left with the responsibility of managing their finances, which they may have never done before. Or worse, they may be left with less than they expected.

Another common hurdle faced by women is the impact of divorce. This is another case where it may be the first time they will handle their finances, or they may receive less in a divorce settlement than anticipated.

Equally important—and sometimes a significant hurdle—is the impact of a second marriage for a woman. It can mean the loss of alimony she previously received from her former spouse, a prenuptial agreement with her new spouse (which may limit access to finances during the marriage or in a subsequent divorce), additional stepchildren with financial needs, and the possibility of financial obligations of her new spouse.

On account of these hurdles and gender differences, women often develop practices that are contrary to the Ten Critical Habits of Truly Rich People. For these reasons, women should pay particularly close attention to the importance of honestly knowing their financial picture (Habit #1), planning for retirement (Habit #6), and discussing money with family, trusted others, and experts (Habits #s 5, 7, and 9).

## THE BLACK WEALTH GAP

Unlike the slowly closing wealth gap for gender, the wealth disparity in this country is staggering between black people and our white counterparts, and it is catastrophic between black women and everyone else. Black people are also often faced with cultural practices that are contrary to the Ten Critical Habits of Truly Rich People.

It is fairly simple to understand the origin of the wealth gap between black people and white people in this country. Slavery was allowed in North America for 246 years, which drove wealth accumulation for white landowners who produced cotton and other agricultural products. They were part of a larger capitalist culture in America, but the labor system they utilized to produce these goods relied on enslaved people. White supremacy, which fueled the system of slavery and its aftermath, allowed for the wealth gap to continue—even for non-slaveholding whites—from Reconstruction through today.

Some examples of the systemic effects impacting and sustaining the wealth gap include exclusion of black people from the GI Bill, redlining practices against black people in housing and financial lending, unequal standards of public education in predominantly black neighborhoods, barriers for black people to higher education (affecting career opportunities), income inequality, and Social Security not covering most black people.

As a result, black Americans today own little, if any, of America's land, create little, if any, of the country's resources, and own barely a fraction of the country's wealth. Evidence of the lasting effects of this system can be seen today in the economic status of black Americans, which remains far behind our white counterparts in terms of income, net worth, homeownership, stock ownership, business entrepreneurship, and other metrics.

For instance, the median income of white families in the US is $76,057, compared to that of black families, which is $45,438. The median net worth of white families in the US is $188,200 compared to that of black families, which is $24,100.[6]

If you deduct the family car and other depreciating assets from net worth, white families have a net worth of $109,156 and black families have a net worth of only $2,410. As you can see, there continues to be a slow rate of catching up for black wealth accumulation.

## MEDIAN HOUSEHOLD INCOME (NATIONAL)

| | |
|---|---|
| Everyone: | $68,703 |
| White: | $76,057 |
| Black: $45,438 (60% of white) | |
| Asian: | $98,174 |
| Hispanic: | $56,113 |

Source: Statista Research Department

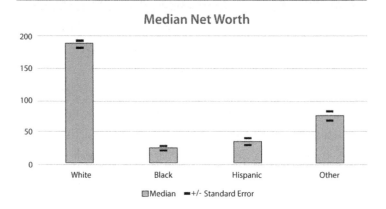

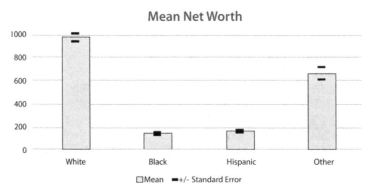

Source: Federal Reserve

## THE HOMEOWNERSHIP GAP

Another significant factor causing the wealth gap is the lack of homeownership. At the end of 2020, the homeownership rate for blacks was at 44%, versus 74% for whites.[7]

This is caused by many factors, including the disparity in income, lack of financial resources, and financial institution lending practices. Lenders deny mortgages for black applicants at a rate 80% higher than that of white applicants.[8] Additionally, by looking at data from the 2019 American Housing Survey (AHS), high-income black homeowners receive higher interest rates than low-income white homeowners. This is critical because the patterns of homeownership by age, race, and ethnicity are similar to wealth patterns.[9]

## INHERITANCE & GENERATIONAL WEALTH GAP

Another reason wealth accumulation is relatively high among white families is they are considerably more likely to have received an inheritance, gift, or other higher level of family support. According to one study, 30% of white families received an inheritance or gift compared to 10% of black families. White families also tend to receive larger inheritances.[10] The study also reveals that bequests and transfers of this type account for more of the racial wealth gap than any other demographic or socioeconomic indicator.

## BLACK WOMEN

Compared to the positive trends for white women and wealth, the state of black women and wealth is significantly behind. As an example, in 2013, the median wealth for single white women in the US was $15,640. Meanwhile, the median wealth for single black women was just $100!

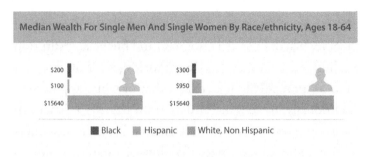

Median Wealth For Single Men And Single Women By Race/ethnicity, Ages 18-64

| | Single Women | | Single Men |
|---|---|---|---|
| Black | $200 | | $300 |
| Hispanic | $100 | | $950 |
| White, Non Hispanic | $15640 | | $15640 |

■ Black    ■ Hispanic    ■ White, Non Hispanic

Source: from 2013 Survey of Consumer Finances data

According to a report published by Goldman Sachs in 2021, America's black women have more than 90% less wealth than American white men. Black women currently earn 15% less than white women and 35% less than white men.[11]

When cognizant of these wealth gaps for black women and black people in general, it should come as no surprise that black Everyday People struggle to achieve financial and emotional wealth.

In addition, as is the case with gender, there are some culturally-based differences and hurdles black people have in this regard. Black people—and black women in particular—often develop practices that are contrary to the Ten Critical Habits of Truly Rich People. For Black women, these are in addition to the gender-based differences and hurdles we also face as women noted above.

## THE INVESTMENT GAP

The differences in the approach to investing by black people as compared to white people are illuminating. Research shows there are far fewer black Americans investing than white Americans, with 61% of whites participating in the stock market versus 28% of blacks.[12] While 18.6% of white households own stocks, only 6.7% of black households do.[13] This racial investment gap is caused by many factors including the disparity in income, lack of financial resources, lack of investing education, and barriers to access.

Studies have shown black Americans are less likely to take financial risks than white Americans. As a result, while investing in equities is a great method to build wealth over time, some black Americans are more conservative in this area.[14]

Finally, white people talk about investing with each other and with their families, but in my experience, black people are less likely to do so. As a result, the investment gap has a cyclical impact—fewer black people invest, and therefore we don't talk about or share information about investing, which leads to less incentive to invest, and so on.

For this reason, black people and people of color should pay particularly close attention to the need for investing (Habit #4) and the importance of discussing money with family, trusted others, and experts (Habit #s 5, 7, and 9).

## THE RETIREMENT SAVINGS GAP

As noted above, black people invest at a lower rate than white people. Retirement accounts are a type of investing and a significant channel through which families accumulate wealth, as well as a source of financial security in retirement. However, not everyone is qualified to enroll in an employer-sponsored retirement plan, which is one explanation for the disparities in retirement account savings.

Many people of color may not be eligible for an employer plan because their company or employer does not offer it, or they are not eligible to participate for other reasons. Additionally, many of America's lowest-paying jobs are filled by black people and other people of color.[15] Those jobs are less likely to come with a 401k retirement plan opportunity. People who lack access to these retirement plan opportunities through employment can also miss out on a common added benefit, which is employer-matched contributions to the plan.

Here are few eye-opening data points about retirement savings:

- The majority of Americans aren't saving enough for retirement, but minorities, in particular, are at greater risk for instability during retirement.

- On average, people of color in the U.S. have less saved for retirement than white people.

- More than half of black and Latinx households have no retirement savings, while only a third of white households lack savings.

- Racial pay gaps lend to black and Latinx workers having lower lifetime earnings and saving less.

- Black and Latinx workers are less likely to work for employers who offer retirement plans.

- A government study showed that black and Latinx savers are more likely to invest in safe assets with lower returns.

- Racial disparities in homeownership and generational wealth also contribute to discrepancies in retirement savings.[16]

For this reason, black people and people of color should pay particularly close attention to the importance of planning for retirement (Habit #6), and the importance of discussing money with family, trusted others, and experts (Habit #s 5, 7, and 9).

## THE ENTREPRENEURIAL GAP

Entrepreneurs will tell you, and I have seen firsthand from my clients, that owning your own business can significantly impact your ability to accumulate wealth. But it often takes wealth to become an entrepreneur.[17] This is why family wealth can contribute to an individual's likelihood to become an entrepreneur. But according to the U.S. Census Bureau, there are only around 124,000 Black-owned businesses with more than one employee, which is only 2% of the nation's closely-held businesses.

Entrepreneurs tend to be white and come from higher-income families. This is because capital is needed to start a business. For many entrepreneurs, capital is created through homeownership and family assets (which has a significant gap for black people). A business that starts out well-funded is more likely to be successful and also more likely to receive additional capital.[18] As a result, black entrepreneurs, on average, launch their businesses with $35,000 in startup capital and loans, versus an average of $107,000 for white entrepreneurs. Additionally, capital for starting a business is often not obtained through traditional lending but through private funding and access to a robust network of wealth.[19] As a result, access to capital is a major barrier to black entrepreneurship, which creates a conundrum, as black business owners are 20% less likely to fund their startups with bank business loans.[20]

For this reason, black people and people of color should pay particularly close attention to credit (Habit #3) and the importance of discussing money with family, trusted others, and experts (Habit #s 5, 7, and 9).

## THE GIVING DISTORTION

Finally, another significant hurdle and cultural difference black people face and which contributes to the development of practices that are contrary to the Ten Critical Habits of Truly Rich People is the way in which we tend to give to others. Despite the significant gaps in income and wealth accumulation, black families prioritize philanthropy more than all racial or ethnic groups, contributing the largest proportion of their wealth—which can include savings, used cars, land, and investment accounts—to charity since 2010. This means that while blacks are significantly behind in accumulating wealth, we are giving the wealth we do accumulate away at a much higher rate than whites.[21]

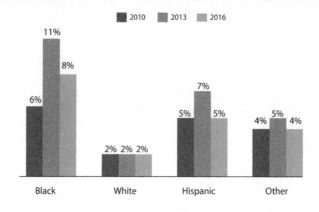

Source: from 2013 Survey of Consumer Finances data

For this reason, black people and people of color should pay particularly close attention to avoiding negative charitable giving tendencies in favor of positive giving and helping others (Habit #s 8 and 10).

As you can see, there are numerous factors women and people of color face which can decrease the odds for our accumulation of wealth and the development of the Ten Critical Habits of Truly Rich People. If we are to become Truly Rich, we must overcome these odds.

# NOTES

## INTRODUCTION:

1. "Credit Suisse Global 2021 Report," Why wealth matters. The Global wealth report., Credit Suisse, accessed October 7, 2021, https://www.credit-suisse.com/media/assets/corporate/docs/about-us/research/publications/global-wealth-report-2021-en.pdf.

## CHAPTER 9:

1. The 2019 Lincoln Retirement Power® Participant Study is based on a national survey of 2,580 full-time workers who have been contributing to their current employers' retirement plans for at least one year. The 2019 Lincoln Retirement Power® Non-participant Study is based on a national survey of 1,008 full- time workers who aren't participating in their employers' plans.

## CHAPTER 12:

1. "Study: It Pays to Be Generous," The Ascent, A Motley Fool Service, accessed October 7, 2021, https://www.fool.com/the-ascent/research/study-it-pays-be-generous/.

## APPENDIX:

1. "The Female Economy," Harvard Business Review, accessed October 7, 2021, https://hbr.org/2009/09/the-female-economy.

2.   "The best travel rewards credit cards of October 2021,
     Insider: Personal Finance, Business Insider, accessed
     October 7, 2021, https://www.businessinsider.com/
     personal-finance/women-now-control-more-than-half-of-
     us-personal-wealth-2015-4.

3.   "Women as the next wave of growth in US wealth
     management," McKinsey & Company Financial
     Services, accessed October 7, 2021, https://www.
     mckinsey.com/industries/financial-services/our-insights/
     women-as-the-next-wave-of-growth-in-us-wealth-
     management.

4.   "Labor Force Statistics from the Current Population
     Survey," U.S. Bureau of Labor Statistics, accessed
     October 7, 2021, https://www.bls.gov/cps/
     cpsaat03.htm.

5.   "Number of Women-Owned Businesses Increased
     Nearly 3,000% since 1972, According to New
     Research," Businesswire, A Berkshire Hathaway
     Company, accessed October 7, 2021, https://www.
     businesswire.com/news/home/20180821005093/en/
     Number-of-Women-Owned-Businesses-Increased-
     Nearly-3000-since-1972-According-to-New-Research.

6.   "Survey of Consumer Finances (SCF)," Board of
     Governors of the Federal Reserve System, Federal
     Reserve, accessed October 7, 2021, https://www.
     federalreserve.gov/econres/scfindex.htm.

7.   "Black homeownership has declined since 2012,"
     MarketWatch, accessed October 7, 2021, https://www.
     marketwatch.com/story/black-homeownership-has-
     declined-since-2012-heres-where-black-households-are-
     most-likely-to-be-homeowners-2020-06-30.

8. "Mortgage data (HMDA)," Consumer Financial Protection Bureau, accessed October 7, 2021, https://www.consumerfinance.gov/data-research/hmda/.

9. "Survey of Consumer Finances (SCF)," Board of Governors of the Federal Reserve System, Federal Reserve, accessed October 7, 2021, https://www.federalreserve.gov/econres/scfindex.htm.

10. "Disparities in Wealth by Race and Ethnicity in the 2019 Survy of Consumer Finances," FEDS Notes, Board of Governors of the Federal Reserve System, Federal Reserve, accessed October 7, 2021, https://www.federalreserve.gov/econres/notes/feds-notes/disparities-in-wealth-by-race-and-ethnicity-in-the-2019-survey-of-consumer-finances-20200928.htm.

11. "Black women's wealth is 90% lower than White men. Goldman Sachs is investing billions to change that," CNN Business, CNN, accessed October 7, 2021, https://www.cnn.com/2021/03/10/investing/black-women-wealth-gap-goldman-sachs/index.html.

12. "Black Americans not investing in the stock market, and it's costing them," The Denver Channel.com National News, accessed October 7, 2021, https://www.thedenverchannel.com/news/national/black-americans-not-investing-in-the-stock-market-and-its-costing-them.

13. "McKinsey Global Institute Special Report, The economic state of Black America: What is and what could be," McKinsey & Company, accessed October 7, 2021, https://www.mckinsey.com/featured-insights/diversity-and-inclusion/the-economic-state-of-black-america-what-is-and-what-could-be.

14. "Black Americans are less likely to invest than white Americans, but experts say 5 steps can change that," Insider Personal Finance, Business Insider, accessed October 7, 2021, https://www.businessinsider.com/personal-finance/how-to-close-racial-investing-gap-2020-9.

15. "Black Americans not investing in the stock market, and it's costing them," The Denver Channel.com National News, accessed October 7, 2021, https://www.thedenverchannel.com/news/national/black-americans-not-investing-in-the-stock-market-and-its-costing-them.; "Disparities in Wealth by Race and Ethnicity in the 2019 Survey of Consumer Finances," FEDS Notes, Board of Governors of the Federal Reserve System, Federal Reserve, accessed October 7, 2021, https://www.federalreserve.gov/econres/notes/feds-notes/disparities-in-wealth-by-race-and-ethnicity-in-the-2019-survey-of-consumer-finances-20200928.htm.

16. "Retirement Savings by Race," Personal Finance - Retirement Planning, Investopedia, accessed October 7, 2021, https://www.investopedia.com/retirement-savings-by-race-5086962.

17. "Does Racial Wealth Disparity Hinder Entrepreneurship?," Currents, Kauffman Foundation, accessed October 7, 2021, https://www.kauffman.org/currents/does-racial-wealth-disparity-hinder-entrepreneurship/; "Smart and Illicit: Who Becomes an Entrepreneur and Do They Earn More?," Working Papers, NBER, accessed October 7, 2021, https://www.nber.org/papers/w19276.

18. ibid

19. "McKinsey Global Institute Special Report, The economic state of Black America: What is and what could be," McKinsey & Company, accessed October 7, 2021, https://www.mckinsey.com/featured-insights/ diversity-and-inclusion/the-economic-state-of-black-america-what-is-and-what-could-be.

20. "Black women's wealth is 90% lower than White men. Goldman Sachs is investing billions to change that," CNN Business, CNN, accessed October 7, 2021, https://www.cnn.com/2021/03/10/investing/black-women-wealth-gap-goldman-sachs/index.html.

21. "Disparities in Wealth by Race and Ethnicity in the 2019 Survy of Consumer Finances," FEDS Notes, Board of Governors of the Federal Reserve System, Federal Reserve, accessed October 7, 2021, https:// www.federalreserve.gov/econres/notes/feds-notes/ disparities-in-wealth-by-race-and-ethnicity-in-the-2019-survey-of-consumer-finances-20200928.htm.; "Despite the racial wealth gap, blackphilanthropy is strong," Urban Wire: Nonprofits and Philanthropy, Urban Institute, accessed October 7, 2021,  https:// www.urban.org/urban-wire/despite-racial-wealth-gap-black-philanthropy-strong.

# ABOUT THE AUTHOR

**N**ICOLE PERKINS is an executive leader with a 30+ year career in Client Advisory Services and Corporate Management. She has extensive experience in wealth management, business strategy and management, talent development and diversity & inclusion.

As a speaker and writer, Nicole speaks to financial matters as well as her unique experiences as a black female executive and mother of multicultural children. Her multi-industry experience spans the financial services, legal, hospitality, entertainment, and communications industries.

Nicole's written work has been featured in *Financial Advisor IQ*, *Philadelphia Business Journal*, *Advisor Magazine*, and Fairygodboss.com. Her speaking engagements include Bloomberg Radio, Financial Planning Association National Conference, and Forum for Executive Women.

Nicole has received recognition for her career accomplishments in numerous publications including, Barron's *Penta* magazine. She was named by *Philadelphia Business Journal* as a 2019 Power Woman in Finance and by *Money Management Executive* as one of the ten winners of the 2018 Top Women in Asset Management, among numerous other recognitions.

Made in the USA
Middletown, DE
24 November 2021

52896552R00106